CALIBAN'S CURSE

Caliban's Curse

GEORGE LAMMING AND THE

REVISIONING OF HISTORY

Supriya Nair

ANN ARBOR

THE UNIVERSITY OF MICHIGAN PRESS

Copyright © by the University of Michigan 1996
All rights reserved
Published in the United States of America by
The University of Michigan Press
Manufactured in the United States of America
⊗ Printed on acid-free paper
1999   1998   1997   1996   4   3   2   1

A CIP catalog record for this book is available from the British Library.

Library of Congress Cataloging-in-Publication Data

Nair, Supriya, 1961–
    Caliban's curse : George Lamming and the revisioning of history /
Supriya Nair.
        p.   cm.
    Includes bibliographical references and index.
    ISBN 0-472-10717-8 (hardcover : alk. paper)
    1. Lamming, George, 1927–   —Knowledge—History.   2. Literature
and history—Caribbean Area.   3. Caribbean Area—In literature.
4. Group identity in literature.   5. West Indians in literature.
I. Title.
PR9230.9.L25Z79   1996
813—dc20   96-10322
                                                            CIP

For Gopalan Nair, Janaki Mundadath, and Sudha

Acknowledgments

If there is an originary moment to this text, it is marked by my introduction to the works of George Lamming through the essays of Ngũgĩ wa Thiong'o. This project gained concrete shape, however, in various seminars with Barbara Harlow. As a doctoral candidate at the University of Texas at Austin, I benefited immensely from her insights. This project owes much to her, even as it has changed through the years. My thanks also to Ann Cvetkovich, Anne Norton, Michael Hanchard, Katie Kane, Laura Lyons, Purnima Bose, and S. Shankar, who have read and commented on earlier versions.

My meetings with George Lamming at the University of Miami did much to re-energize and confirm my sense of direction. He graciously made time for me in spite of a busy schedule and was such a fascinating conversationalist that I almost missed my return flight. I can only hope that this critical appreciation of his work demonstrates his productive influence over my own thinking.

I am indebted to a great many people in the later stages of this work as well. Janice Carlisle painstakingly yet swiftly read and helped me reconceptualize the manuscript against looming deadlines, and she, along with Joseph Roach, Maaja Stewart, Geoffrey Harpham, Teresa Toulouse, Richard Rambuss, Rebecca Mark, Amy Koritz, Felipe Smith, and Catherine Den Tandt, provided the collegial friendship without which academic work would be hollow. Errol and Grace Hill, Bernth Lindfors, Abiola Irele, Isaac Mowoe, Lupenga Mphande, and John

Conteh-Morgan provided various professional and personal avenues for productive discussions that ultimately facilitated revision. The two anonymous readers offered critical readings that were very helpful. A Tulane Committee on Research Award made possible an additional summer of revision. My upbeat and energetic editor, LeAnn Fields, always knew just what to say to keep the momentum going. My thanks also to Kelly Sippell for her help during the copyediting stage.

For being a partner in the most ideal sense of the term, my thanks to Gaurav Desai. Rajan, Sanjeevan, Suresh, and Madhaven Nair must take credit for nurturing my love for reading. For years of support bordering on dangerous indulgence, I thank Sudha and Shree Kumar. And, as always, no enterprise of mine has ever been complete without the solid, dependable foundation of my parents, whose generosity never ceases to amaze me.

Contents

Introduction

George Lamming's "Occasion for Speaking"

And when the Priest has found his powers, the dead come forward. You don't see them; but they will be there, and you can hear them. They speak about all the things that had never been said when they were alive. They are now free to accuse, and free to pardon. And the living must reply.
  —George Lamming, *Water With Berries*

On June 21, 1980, an angry group of mourners at a Guyanese church observed a "white-hair man with a accent" deliver his eulogy after a series of other eulogies had been heard.[1] The occasion: the funeral of Walter Rodney, one of the most promising activists from an area that has had its fair share of brilliant modern intellectuals. The speaker: George Lamming, the writer from Barbados, who had made the trip to Guyana in order to pay tribute to a respected colleague from the Caribbean. The irony: Rodney's body was absent from the church. The authorities had refused to release his remains for the funeral after he was assassinated on June 13, 1980, in Georgetown, Guyana. At the time of his death, Rodney was perceived as a major oppositional voice to the ruling elites of Guyana; an already distrustful populace imagined the worst. The atmosphere in the church was understandably simmering. By the time Lamming had concluded his eulogy, however, he had roused the initially hostile and suspicious audience, many of whom were members of the Working People's Alliance (WPA) Party, to a standing ovation. Lamming spoke briefly but passionately of Rodney's murder, attributing his untimely death "to a long, long, tradition of nightmare and terror which has always been at the heart of the history of these Americas."[2] His eulogy made no reference to the fact that Rodney's body was not present. And to the mourners, Rodney, it seemed, had momentarily returned in spirit.

Lamming's performance in the church on that bleak day in June admirably characterizes his perception of his task not just as an orator but also as a writer. Locating an individual act of killing within a historical legacy, he refuses to be silenced by the inheritance of violence. For those critics wearied by the colonizer-colonized classifications, Lamming's attempt to seek continuity with the history of colonialism might seem to run the risk of simply repeating its dominant paradigms when we might as well move on to a discourse, if not a practice, beyond "What Europe Did" and "What Europe Did Next." But for a writer who was trained more thoroughly in the British literary canon than in any indigenous one, and whose conventional British colonial education eased him into the literary circles of London in the early fifties, the conditions under which he first began writing in what was then commonly called the West Indies[3] made it impossible for him to bypass the colonial period. In historicizing these conditions of possibility, this book attempts to locate George Lamming within the debates among those primarily "anglophone" Caribbean writers whose explorations of the colonial question continue to resonate in contemporary debates about writing in the Caribbean and in the field of postcolonial studies in general. Significantly, a recent major postcolonial reader begins with an excerpt from Lamming's collection of essays, *The Pleasures of Exile*, aptly titled "The Occasion for Speaking."[4]

In "The Occasion for Speaking,"[5] originally published in 1960, Lamming discusses one of the most familiar debates about the Caribbean that is both specific to the region and representative of the colonies in general: the question of history. Particularly since V. S. Naipaul reaffirmed the dismissive statements of J. Anthony Froude, debates about the historical potential of the Caribbean have raged loud and long.[6] But Lamming's position on this issue is unique among his contemporaries in his interpretation not so much of what constitutes history and who are the instruments of its achievement, but of how it is that literature itself contributes to the ambitious enterprise of the making of history. Lamming does not always read history conventionally as significant events exclusive of everyday life; rather, he sees literature as a kind of imaginative record that paradoxically substantiates and challenges historical narratives. In Lamming's work, creative writing and history appear as symbionts, dependent upon each other. But he makes fiction the primary site, forcing its close neighbor to alter its course. Rather than respectfully abide by the rules of institutionalized history, Lamming deploys antihistorical tendencies, along with the license allowed by literary conventions, in order to push history—narrative as well as event—in new directions.

Despite the fact that Lamming's own focus is on beginnings rather than on endings, on an open future rather than a closed one, his provocative challenge to hasty terminal signposts of historical progress or failure is addressed in a teleological scheme of its own. "Occasion" begins by declaring that it was a miracle to have any West Indian writers at all, given the almost complete lack of encouragement at home, but finally gives a place of honor to the West Indian novel, claiming that it is the third significant historical event in the modern Caribbean, the first being Columbus's entry and the second being the abolition of slavery and the arrival of Indian and Chinese laborers (36–37). As his novels demonstrate, the primacy he gives Columbus here does not indicate that anything before the so-called discovery of the Indies was insignificant. But it does emphasize Lamming's perception of the Caribbean as repopulated and manufactured, more than any other site of imperial dominance, as first and foremost a colony. Although he plots the schematic framework within a colonial succession that is initiated with Columbus, Lamming uses the third event to displace and trouble the complacency of the first. He argues that what "the West Indian has to do if he is going to be released from this prison of colonialism, from this dread of standing up, is precisely what the whole world is now called upon to do. . . . For the West Indies . . . belong to that massive peasant majority whose leap in the twentieth century has shattered all the traditional calculations of the West, of European civilization" (36).

Since, in Lamming's view, the Caribbean novel has had a major role to play in giving voice to the peasant struggles that overset the predicted trajectory of dominant, that is, Western history (except in a Marxist formulation) and that were primarily responsible for challenging colonial dominance, it is not surprising that he gives precedence to the novelist over the historian. While most historians were tracking traditional narratives of Western bourgeois history, many Caribbean novelists, according to Lamming, were already disrupting those very same narratives through frontal attacks on the colonialist assumptions behind their construction. "They [the novelists] are the first builders of what will become a tradition in West Indian imaginative writing," says Lamming, making a prediction of his own about the fundamental importance of peasant life in any story about the islands (38). The novelist therefore traces a definite connection between the resistance to colonialism, among other systems of oppression, embodied in the peasant uprisings and the fictional writing that was inspired by these struggles. Although he later backed off from his criticism of John Hearne, who, he charges, broke from this supposedly "authentic" Caribbean tradition by focusing too much on the agricultural middle class, Lamming continues to insist on the rural poor as a defining impetus to the organic ideal of his cultural work.[7] And while one can argue with his essentialist notion of peasant consciousness and the primacy of what is predominantly a middle-class genre in its expression, the import of peasant revolts is integral to his conception of history and to his theory of literature's impact on it.

What Sidney Mintz calls "the first overseas agricultural factories of Europe" were assembled in the Caribbean through the cultural determinants not only of class, but also of race. Plantation labor was largely black, and even after Emancipation in Barbados, Lamming's native island, peasant labor continued to be largely black. The alienation that Lamming reads into skin color as a basis of class identity in his first novel, *In the Castle of My Skin,* intimately connects landlessness and lack of stable identity or concrete history with the established conventions of racism. But as Lamming demonstrates in the novel, peasant riots erupted into the national scene, resisting both colonialist and emerging nationalist support of a racialized class hierarchy. In fact, Mintz argues that the mere formation of peasant communities in the Caribbean was itself a sign of resistance because they often functioned in defiance of the structures of slavery, metropolitan dominance, and plantation economy that had previously held sway. Although Mintz cautions against homogenizing the complex makeup of rural life on the islands, he nevertheless seems in general agreement with Lamming (whom he quotes at the beginning of his own essay on the Caribbean region) that the establishment of rural proletariats "was, after the Haitian Revolution and subsequent emancipation elsewhere, the single most important sociological fact in Caribbean life in the nineteenth century." Since agricultural labor was the base of the "foreign invention"[8] of Caribbean plantation society, Lamming's insistence on foregrounding the foundation from the inside seeks to rewrite a literally manufactured history of imposition and dispossession.

Clearly, Lamming includes the role of capital in the genesis of modern Caribbean society as part of his larger critique of social practices that debased human labor. His scrupulous attention to the past as a necessary intervention into the future also makes it impossible for him to avoid the colonial structures that underwrote the contemporary social formations, and, in fact, impels him to make explicit connections between colonialism and capitalism. The past is therefore crucial to him, not just in providing an explanation for the current position of the self in society, but also, with that knowledge, in transforming the relationship of the self to the social domain. The structural determinants of society are not reified but become open to human agency, and from Lamming's perspective, the peasants in the Caribbean are primarily responsible for change as agents of collective action. But such movements do not pave the way for a grand revolution; instead, they appear as a momentary flash in the flow of everyday life. Lamming's fourth novel, *Season of Adventure*, charts a brief but timely disruption of a neocolonial regime, which has a significant political impact but refuses to promise more than a seasonal, local transformation. While the material aspect of social organization seems threatened by the organic, impersonal cycles of nature, the novel emphasizes human engagement with the natural and social environment, even if it disavows ultimate control. The brutal history of the islands, bemoaned by Naipaul, cannot yet be overcome, but that past is redeemed for Lamming by the historical emergence of the peasants as a national force.

Upon discovering the "theft" of proletarian subjectivity, in becoming conscious of one's position as commodity, as J. M. Bernstein, citing Georg Lukács, puts it, "commodity relations themselves become self-conscious, that is, they come to know themselves for what they are: social relations between men submerged in the guise of quantitative relations between things." Bernstein goes on to say of this self-consciousness about commodification that the "meaning in the social experience of a class attempting to make sense of its social placement . . . is historical; it is *the* meaning of history." While Lamming would not subscribe to a singular meaning of history based solely on class, he would agree with Bernstein that history becomes philosophical when the awareness of social placement stimulates revolutionary praxis.[9] An important imperative behind a historical consciousness is the recognition of one's value or worth as human being, which, according to Lamming, eventually makes one conscious of one's current position and stimulates the desire to change it.

Where is the novelist's place in witnessing the enactment of philosophical history or, as Bernstein prefers, in interpreting the meaning of history when it seems to become accessible? Acknowledging Richard Wright's comments on Lamming's first novel, in which Wright reads *In the Castle* as a symbolic representation of worldwide peasant movements in the twentieth century, Lamming goes on to use the language not of seasonal change, but of militant struggle in the villages. "This is the most fundamental battle of our time, and I am joyfully lucky to have been made, by my work, a soldier in their ranks," he declares. Lamming maps out diasporic connections not only with Wright, but with Ngũgĩ wa Thiong'o, the Kenyan novelist who claimed to have been inspired by reading Lamming and saw *In the Castle* as "the signal which alerted him to what he had to do as a Kikuyu and pan-Africanist writer. . . ."[10] Ngũgĩ's specific experience with colonial education and his childhood in a Gikuyu village made Lamming's work stimulate a political conversion in his own pedagogical and artistic interests that eventually led to his choosing to work on Lamming while he was a student at Leeds in the sixties. Ngũgĩ's sense of learning from the work of Lamming supports Henry Louis Gates's critique of the fetishized status of Frantz Fanon as the sole representative voice of the so-called Third World. The explicit connection across diasporic spaces points to a multiplicity of voices speaking from the vast terrain of the Third World and to their interconnectedness.[11]

Ngũgĩ's distance from the Gikuyu peasants as a result of an education that granted him mobility in class status and alienated him from the direct experience of peasant life, including the use of their language, must qualify the sense of committment articulated by both these writers. While Lamming might see himself as a soldier in the ranks of the peasants, he nevertheless operates from a very different location in culture. He is not blind to the tensions of articulating a coherent national identity, as all his novels show, since his refusal to construct a unified narrator comes from the impossibility of creating a unified national subject that can claim to speak for diverse groups. Even as *In the Castle* strives toward a communal identity based first on class and later on race, neither project is successful.

The risks of claiming representative status, in speaking for subaltern groups, as against naming them, are apparent in Lamming's emphasis on the significance of the Caribbean novel.[12] Forgetting, it seems, his own warnings about class distinctions, Lamming declares that "it is the West Indian novel that has restored the West Indian peasant to his true and original status of personality" (*Pleasures,* 39). His later comments on the Caribbean novel are more carefully worded and nuanced, although they continue to generalize the pervasiveness of peasant influence and its relation to "the supreme concern of the total society." He amends the earlier assertion to put the emphasis more appropriately on the transformation in the audience rather than in the subjects themselves: "fiction has served as a way of restoring these lives—this world of men and women down below—to a proper order of attention" (*Castle,* xxxvii).

While Lamming insists on fiction in the final instance as more effectively performing the task that should have been the historian's, he does not neglect the role of particular intellectuals who have been influential in revisionist histories of the "world of men and women down below." *The Pleasures of Exile,* specifically, contests a classic literary trope through C. L. R. James's *Black Jacobins,* which Lamming initially calls essential "Bible-reading," although he takes James to task later for getting carried away with the heroics of his protagonist.[13] Lamming's analysis in "Caliban Orders History," another essay in *The Pleasures,* extends a literary character to fit the historical figure of Toussaint L'Ouverture, one of the leaders of the Haitian Revolution in 1791 and the primary figure in James's book. James, he says, "shows us Caliban as Prospero had never known him: a slave who was a great soldier in battle, an incomparable administrator in public affairs; full of paradox but never without compassion, a humane leader of men" (119). In thus collating the disciplines, Lamming not only underlines the cooperation between them in colonialist fictions, which were passed off as historical facts, but also conversely suggests ways in which one discipline can illuminate our "way of seeing," to use his phrase, another. The historical persona of Toussaint reinvents the stereotypical savage in Shakespeare's *The Tempest,* rendering a familiar interpretation of the play suspect by transferring the possibilities of the Haitian Revolution into the realm of fictional drama. But in making so intimate an incorporation of history into literature, Lamming also disrupts the scientific or factual

claims of history, a disruption that is shared by James's polemical confrontation with the imperial version of the Haitian Revolution that dismissed the troublesome, former slave, Toussaint.

In similarly foregrounding the narrativization of history and
demonstrating that there were high stakes involved in who got to control the narrative, both of these writers expose the fallacy of disinter-
ested reportage and apolitical fiction. As it turns out, Lamming goes on
to imply that neither mainstream history nor literature, both complici-
tous narratives in the colonial process, will serve the purpose he has
outlined for the Caribbean novel. Eurocentric and bourgeois in perspective, as well as racially limited in inclusiveness, the inherited,
canonical traditions of these two terrains fall short of capably handling
the challenges they face in such contentious discourse.

In tracing slave revolt in the early colonial history of Haiti, when
property began to see itself "as a source of possibility," Lamming
argues, "some new sight as well as some new sense of language is
required to bear witness to the miracle." The image he uses to depict
this transformation is that of a plow that refuses to plow, but instead
somersaults into a reverse position and directs its "ten points of steel"
threateningly at those who have appropriated it as mindless property
(*Pleasures*, 121). He is, of course, thinking of the reversal of the slave
against the master, but in his own context the image applies to the peasants as well. The demand for a new vision as well as a new narrative
style to capture the momentous change inspires Lamming's unique
sense of the form and function of literature. Incorporating the traditions
of conventional fictional narrative—plot, theme, image, irony, and so
on—the novelist brings his previous experience in writing poetry and
his commitment to a political agenda to bear on his works. But he uses
the mechanism of the realist novel only as a point of departure, putting
pressure on all the familiar narrative strategies by introducing not only
his distinct prose style, but also what he sees as Caribbean influences
into the structural and stylistic framework of a borrowed literary tradition.

The oral traditions of the villagers, for instance, embodied in various characters and often replayed in the dramatic and poetic dialogues
that constantly break up the prose, define the world of *In the Castle*.
Hence Pa's dream vision, which is recited rather than narrated, allows
us a glimpse of the obscured past of slavery that the prosaic narrator
refuses to supply. But the provision is made late into the text—a char-

acteristic deferral of a narrative complement to the schoolboys' mystified whispers about the slave past. And in another characteristic fusion, the historical present of the riots in the novel precedes the almost mythicized presentation of the slave trade, which, although belated, begins to make sense when one notes its position in a chapter that opens by remarking how little has changed since the riots. That mundane observation soon leaps into Pa's dream, and the prose dissolves into a prophetic rendering of continuing diasporic fragmentation, situating the slavers and the slaves as the predecessors of Creighton, Slime, and the other characters:

> Now there's been new combinations and those that come after make quite a different collection. So if you hear some young fool fretting about back to Africa, keep far from the invalid and don't force a passage to where you won't yet belong. These words not for you but those that come after. . . . From part of you that's neither flesh nor bone in a sleep before your last and longest, I come to say what I say. (211)

The passage combines a number of typical themes in Lamming's work: the formation of diaspora; the metaphorical connection to Africa that must nevertheless be differentiated from the Caribbean, where one now belongs; the haunted and haunting past and its ethical imperative for the future; the "occasion for speaking" and its ambivalence toward history. Its placement in the text, almost at its conclusion, also illustrates the back-and-forth time scheme through which the narrative unfolds, a movement that is characteristic of Lamming's novels.

Significantly, the eventual disclosure of the repressed slave past in *In the Castle* does not pretend to the factuality or realist traditions of either the historical treatise or the realist novel. Lamming is not interested in writing a historical novel so much as in playing with the disciplinary authority of history and the realist status of the literary narrator. Nor is the "real" of any particular use to him, even in a materialist sense, except as a social construction that must be critiqued within the confines of fiction. Perhaps "confines" may not be the mot juste here, since Lamming seems to see fiction as a liberation from the tyrannical constraints of history as it has been used in the Caribbean.

Lamming is not by any means actually arguing for the complete irrelevance of history in the Caribbean, but rather, using fictional modes, he invents traditions, in the sense that Eric Hobsbawm uses the phrase, to remake a past that humanizes his ancestors.[14] Since contemporary historiography has been informed, like anthropology, through the Western encounter with the "other" that must be posited, in the first case, as being without history, the writing of history is challenged by other kinds of discourse, including fiction, that perversely appropriate the act of writing to claim historicity. The blank page of the New World upon which Western desire was written is found to be not empty so much as emptied of its previous content.[15] Reinscribing what has been lost is a difficult task when the usual methods of documentation have been denied, so writing goes beyond rediscovery to invention.

In one of his interviews, Lamming outlines one aspect of resistance in the process of speaking up. Describing the Moyne Commission hearings at Queen's Park in Barbados after the riots in the thirties, the writer recollects a scene he witnessed as a young boy. Unable to contain the crowds that showed up, the investigatory committees contrived by the colonial administration allowed the proceedings to be broadcast through microphones. While the testimony carried on within the space of Queen's Park, it was frequently interrupted by the crowd on the outskirts calling out in antiphonic, if discordant, response: "Liar! Liar!"[16] What Fanon would call the disruptive "complete calling in[to] question" of colonial accounts is detailed in Lamming's fiction as an initial step.[17] Hence, like many other postcolonial works, a murder mystery, a trial, an investigation, or a quest are frequent plot devices in the novels. But beyond the occasion of murder, exceeding the queries about who killed the dead, is the strong sense of history itself on trial, of its testimony constantly being arrested by charges of mendacity. In many of Lamming's novels, the jury is still out, perhaps because not only are the crimes too numerous, but as he himself asserts, he operates "on the fundamental belief that there are no degrees of innocence" (*Pleasures*, 11). Besides, what concrete judgment can be made on the grounds of irrevocably distorted evidence and when the key witnesses have been disposed of, many of them drowning, shackled to each other, in the mute waters of the sea?

But neither the silence of death nor the untruths of history prevent some things from being heard in the occasion for speaking provided by the fictional imagination. And therein lies the second mode of resistance that surpasses accusation and proceeds to fabricate, quite deliberately, its own account of an alternative sequence. Personalizing the quarrel detailed above with an abstract colonial history, Lamming points to the Haitian Ceremony of the Souls as a way of resolving family quarrels after one or more of the participants have died. Through the ritual of calling upon spirits of the dead to speak through the living, the past is reactivated in the present. "The symbolic function of the ceremony for me, as an artist within the Caribbean situation, is the necessity of reconciling the past with each moment of conscious living," he says.[18] The use of the imagination demanded by this ritual ultimately applies to more than filiation and suturing of domestic bonds. Vodoun emerges as a practice defined by the restrictions of colonial taboos on communal worship, and in reanimating the dead, who speak to and through the living descendants, it revives the trial of colonial history and presents new and unusual evidence. No claims of certainties can be made in the circumstances, but the resurrection is by no means invalid when what has been given the status of absolute truth is revealed also to be based on a spectral past and on long-deceased arbitrators who speak through the body of a text. When no arrangement is made to hear all sides, Lamming seems to think that one must make room for irregular evidence on the part of those who have been excluded. Speculating, for instance, about what the absent Sycorax and Miranda's unnamed mother might have told us in *The Tempest* that might counter Prospero's version, he says provocatively that "our knowledge must be postponed until some arrangement comparable to the Haitian Ceremony of Souls returns them to tell us what we should and ought to know" (*Pleasures*, 116).[19]

Allowing ourselves to ascribe life to the unreal and the dead, whether in the pages of fiction or in the narrative of history, gives a supplementary position to irrational discourse that destabilizes claims of rationalist accounts in history. Paul Ricoeur's formulation of the imagination as a creative and critical interrogation of the domain of reason effectively sums up Lamming's strategy. Remaking reality for both of these intellectuals leads to praxis in the ways articulated by Lamming's image of the plow aggressively coming to life, for, as Ricoeur puts it, "what certain fictions redescribe is precisely human action itself."[20] Although imagination has been largely marginalized in the Western philosophical tradition, especially in its perceived inferior status to reason, several Caribbean writers have made imagination a central constituent of their philosophy. Indeed, Wilson Harris forcefully declares, "I believe a philosophy of history may well lie buried in the arts of the imagination."[21]

Harris is responding to the same pressures that result in Lamming embodying personhood in a plow, the metonymic representation of reified slaves and peasants who implicitly come to consciousness of their humanity. Just as humans *without* property are coterminous with humans *as* property in *In the Castle*, Harris believes that "[p]rison and person had become locked together as uniform property" in accounts of the Caribbean. The violence lies not just in the body being objectified, but as a consequence of that objectification, in the body being torn and transported from its culture and treated like a commodity that has no control over its eventual location. Harris refuses to grant complete mastery to the displacement of slavery, emphasizing instead the "reconstitution" of transplanted and dismembered bodies/histories. Using the material practice of the limbo dance aboard a slave ship, he translates the necessary elasticity of the performance into a general theory of Caribbean cultures.[22] Not forgetting that the parameters of the limbo performance were circumscribed by the cramped and anguished space of the Middle Passage, Harris uses the chronotope, in the Bakhtinian sense, of the slave ship to indicate communal manipulation of an intransigent history. To read more broadly, the confining stasis of imperial history is not negated as a necessary component of the modern Caribbean, but while its weight limits the possibility of movement, the uniformity of objectification is disrupted by the dynamic struggle to be in control of one's motion.[23]

In drawing upon the images of the plow and of Vodoun, of reacting and speaking back, Lamming is unable to reject entirely the formative influence of colonialism. Writing his novels, it must be remembered, mainly between the fifties and the seventies, Lamming makes no apology about his central focus. Neither does he seem to think that a reassessment of the colonial process is somehow a tiresome overstatement that runs the risk of recentralizing Europe. Indeed, to overlook its impact would be a dangerous oversight. As Lamming says in an interview,

> just because the so-called colonial situation and its institutions may have been transferred into something else, it is a fallacy to think that the human-lived content of those situations are automatically transferred into something else, too. The experience is a

continuing psychic experience that has to be dealt with . . . long
after the actual colonial situation formally ends.[24]

As far as Lamming is concerned, it is too soon to call a complete closure
on the colonial situation. But it would also be a mistake to assume that
his concern for past damage traps him forever in what he calls the
"backward glance." His urgent desire to conceive of an occasion for
speaking against the structures of colonialism is informed not just by
the past but by the future as well. Lamming's review of colonial history
asserts the conditions for speaking as constantly subject to change, but
speak one must if one is to move on. As he says in *Pleasures* of the Ceremony of the Souls,

> The Dead need to speak if they are going to enter that eternity
> which will be their last and permanent Future. The living demand
> to hear whether there is any need for forgiveness, for redemption
> . . . their ambitions point to a similar end. They are interested in
> their Future. (9–10)

Moreover, Lamming's Marxist affiliations impel him to go beyond
the psychic emphasis that consumes much of Harris's theories of the
imagination.[25] His work theorizes the cultural force of the imagination
as material phenomenon as well, often using psychic energy as a guide
to concrete social action. For Lamming, Africa fulfills a role in the Afro-
Caribbean imagination similar to that of Hamlet's ghost, illustrating his
primary use of the spiritual as guidance toward action in the material
world.[26] In other instances, though, apparitions and hallucinations are
part of grasping the terror of history, paralyzing rather than initiating
action. If the sense of divine benevolence orders the Hegelian reading
of history, Lamming's frequently melancholic endings that record
abysmal failures profane such historical faith.[27]

Not entirely abandoning the gods, however, Lamming and Harris
valorize Vodoun as a practice that also articulates a reassembly of violated gods, a remaking of scraps of memory into newly created forms.
In seeking to overcome the view of the Caribbean as a space ultimately
crushed by its brutal history of slavery and colonialism, they emphasize the notion of an inspired creativity within impoverished and constrained cultures. Likewise, Derek Walcott's Nobel lecture opens with
the cane effigy of a Hindu god, made in the aptly named village of

"Felicity," to mark the moment of communal celebration.[28] In other words, out of severed bodies and fragmented memories, Walcott explains, in an echo of Harris's limbo concept, the descendants of East Indian laborers portray the remaking of Caribbean culture by its diverse inhabitants. Out of the wreck of history, figuratively represented by the supine and skeletal (cane) god, pieced together in remembrance of interrupted traditions that reappear in the elsewhere of forced migration, new traditions are created and celebrated. Although Walcott seems to have moved away from his earlier critique of worshipping "dead gods"[29] and recognizes the symbolic nature of diasporic connection among the Indians through religion, he does not forget to add that the effigy is ultimately burned. The felicitous ceremony is not a static gaze into history, the "Medusa of the New World," to use Walcott's phrase, and it skirts the dangers of being overwhelmed by the sense of an unheroic, nonproductive history as well as, conversely, a nostalgic homage to one's past.[30] The return is always momentary, a recurral that is eventually a renewal, never quite a cycle that completes itself, but one that turns away from its point of entry.

Lamming seems, for the most part, equally concerned with a critical deployment of the imagination, but unlike Walcott, who declines to put history on the dock because it gave him the "gift" of belonging to the mixed heritage of the Caribbean, Lamming refuses to absolve colonial history. Each of his novels is therefore a militant intervention into a particular phase of colonialism, in a dialogic encounter with both historical and literary accounts of its passage. Dividing the chapters of this study into two interrelated sections, titled "Voyages" and "Intellectuals" respectively, I borrow a common structure in Lamming's novels to emphasize his primary concerns with the migrant intellectual. Although *Natives of My Person* (1972) is so far his most recent novel, I use it as the defining focus of the first chapter since it represents the moment that Lamming describes as the point of entry in "Occasion." As I have said earlier, any sense of rigid chronology of colonial "progress" is disrupted within the narrative structure of this novel in spite of particular historical phases that Lamming appropriates and puts a different spin on, quite literally, through confusing time schemes and the proliferation of chopped narratives. Since my project focuses less on the biographical specificities of Lamming-as-individual-writer and more on the social concerns and dialogues with other writers that direct his work, my departure from a chronological exposition of his novels as they were published is a necessary one. In following the precedent of the single-author work, I break many of its accepted conventions, particularly the depiction of biographical and fictional processes of development. Not simply a dictate of my analytical imperatives, this procedure respects Lamming's own stress on the writer in the social world. Indeed, when a long overdue collection of his essays, addresses, and interviews was published recently, Lamming himself, reveals one of the editors of the volume, chose to title it *Conversations*.[31] While he responds to the issues he examines in his own distinct style, that is, I have found, how best to read Lamming: in conversation with the multiple traditions and influences that inform his work and give it its densely woven texture.

The dialogue is not always a congenial one. Borrowing from Hakluyt's voyages and other colonialist accounts of the initial forays into the New World,[32] Lamming eventually displaces their authority in *Natives* by taking possession of their voices and deflating them through irony and parody. The allegorical play on forms of empire ultimately makes allegory itself a shaky terrain, in which the power of these forms as structured by allegory is denied absolute foundation and is instead constantly deconstructed. The numerous references to faulty vision add to the disconcerting medley of voices and, as Lamming suggests, they do not provide a reasonable ground for an authoritarian narrative. However, the explicit and implicit critique of imperial arrogance does exercise critical judgment, leaving one in no doubt of the novelist's ethical stance toward colonialism.

The second chapter continues to deal with migration, now elaborated in the period between preindependence and neocolonialism. Focusing on *The Emigrants* (1954), his second novel, and *Water With Berries* (1971), his fifth, I argue that the "monomania"[33] of the Caliban trope ultimately makes Lamming's continued critique of forms associated with colonial narratives problematic. Written in response to the modern migration to the English metropolis, both novels counter the notion of the "pleasures of exile" and present a neurotic world that seems to whirl out of control. Lamming himself argues that the almost unbroken bleakness of these novels is meant to suggest not the "death of the West Indian," but "the death of empire," although it detonates amidst the migrants, who cannot escape the devastation.[34] But the most vulnerable victims of the battle in the heart and entrails of the empire are very often women. Men do not fare much better, but women are often the targets of the male characters driven insane by the pressures, not the pleasures, of exile in England. While Lamming critiques some of the characters for their misguided violence, others, such as Teeton and the overseer in *Water With Berries,* are presented sympathetically. Caliban's curse moves beyond the discursive shriek to actual violence, but in Lamming's complex rewriting, much of this action achieves a not always productive completion.

Lamming uses fictional autobiography in his first novel, *In the Castle of My Skin* (1953), to portray the consequences of an education that has almost entirely repressed the slave trade he subjects to scrutiny in *Natives.* In the second section of this study, I deal with issues concerning Lamming's exposition of the responsibility of intellectual engagement with the colonial situation. Although all his works are related to social responsibility, the novels explicated in this section most coherently present issues regarding intellectual leadership and the people it claims to represent. It should be clear at the outset that while Lamming might make distinctions between leaders and the masses, he makes no such distinction between intellectuals and the people. In his eulogy, he says of Walter Rodney that "he was an intellectual in the sense that all men and women are intellectuals. For to be alive is to have a concept, a view of life, to be engaged in or be condemned to making a choice about your actions."[35] This formulation of the intellectual is very similar to Antonio Gramsci's inclusive theory that claims everyone is an intellectual, although some are functionally characterized by their intellectual tasks.[36] In a lecture titled "Western Education and the Caribbean Intellectual," Lamming begins with a quotation from Gramsci that indicates his interest in the way education has shaped intellectuals who have assumed leadership of their societies.[37]

My third chapter explores the architectural and biological implications of the title of his first novel, *In the Castle of My Skin,* borrowed from a poem by Derek Walcott, to situate peasant revolt in the thirties. Dispossession extends from actual housing conditions to one's place in history, and the interiority of the novel's various narrative perspectives looks out from the defining contours of dark skin and landlessness. But just as in the case of movement through limbo, the barriers of identity construction ultimately are stretched and split through the riots that break out in protest. They cannot confine the peasants in the roles prescribed to them.

In this analysis, I describe Lamming's discursive strategies as both emanating from and challenging his own politics. Thus, while strongly identifying with the landless peasants, the novel both begins and ends with the narrative perspective of an alienated G., who is distanced at first by the burden of a grim history and later by the advantages of colonial education. But the narrative style is characteristically layered. As Sandra Pouchet Paquet says of the novel, "The intertwining and overlap of distinct narrative modes intensifies the dramatic contrast between the self-referential quality of the first person narrative and the broader social, historical, and cultural contexts of the third person narrative."[38] The narrative follows G.'s attempt to make sense of his place in the village and to suggest, in Trumper's interventions, individual responsibility for the collective situation of the village.

Learning and revolutionary praxis are often placed in an interactive position. *Water With Berries* posits the return of the alienated intellectual to the islands as a necessary step in the narrative of colonial history. But does the return herald the happy conjunction of the prodigal migrant with those who have stayed behind and the triumphant result of such a progressive embrace? In my fourth chapter, I use Lamming's third and fourth novels, *Season of Adventure* (1960) and *Of Age and Innocence* (1958), to explore the nationalist phase and its consequences in neocolonialism, already predicted in his first novel. Leadership issues conflict with conditions of alienation through colonial education, with the migration to England, and with interracial rivalry in *Of Age*. But Lamming continues to expand on the relationship between narrative and event. Using the legend of the Tribe Boys, who battle the Bandit Kings in an allegorical replay of colonial events, he draws links between the early resistance to colonial traders and settlers and its later manifestations against neocolonial leadership.[39] Whereas *Season* focuses largely on the black populations battling new and corrupt ruling elites, *Of Age* makes San Cristobal, a fictional space often used in his novels, an island more similar to Trinidad, with its multiple races and consequent tensions. The latter novel also locates continuities and discontinuities, not just between one system of colonial hierarchy and another, but between the older and younger generations, as implied by the title. While the older leaders self-destruct as a result of an inability to work together, their progeny, Bob, Singh, and Lee, standing for three major national groups, Afro-Caribbean, Indian, and Chinese, struggle to maintain their close friendship and plan an agenda for the future.

It is to the younger generation that Lamming delivers the task of a different kind of education from the colonial one, suggesting that the problems related to neocolonial structures are yet to be resolved among their parents' generation. In *Pleasures,* the author presents a revised excerpt from and attending explanation to *Of Age.* In an uncanny reversal of the last line of *Natives,* in which the Lady mournfully observes, "we are a future they must learn," here another Lady is shown as being educated by the story of the Tribe Boys, disseminated by the children:

> "Who are these Tribe Boys," the Lady asks.
> "'Tis some history 'bout San Cristobal," says Bob. "We learn it from early."
> "An' if any strangers around," said Singh, "sometimes we tell it as a work. 'Cause not everybody know how to tell it."
> The Lady takes a seat and the face of China like the face of India glances a boy's message to the face of Africa. They are not going to miss this chance. (18–19)

Lamming situates his own tale, like that of the boys, as a "work" of labor offered to those who do not yet know of an almost extinct civilization, the vestiges of which remain in the legends and lore of the later survivors. Like Wilson Harris, Lamming considers legends and fables to be the work of the imagination and he offers them as a creative alternative to the distorted history of the Caribbean.

Season of Adventure is the single novel that stages a completed revolt, although it is only briefly revolutionary. The inventions of the imagination combined in the practice of Vodoun, the drumming on the Reserve, Chiki's painting, and Fola's activism forcefully intervene in the affairs of government, making explicit the effect of art on the transaction of state procedures. Although the novel seems to run the risk of romanticizing the subversive potential of subcultures, it must be noted that overturning one corrupt regime does not foreclose the possibility of yet another one taking over. Nor is art isolated in its scope for transformation. Labor is set in a larger context in which different forms of production mingle into an explosive alloy, gaining hegemony over the earlier state structure in what approaches a Marxist conquest of the state. However, the drummers on the Reserve, the factory workers, the fishermen, and the various other subaltern groups that join hands are not the ones who take over state leadership. Some sense of the vanguard persists in the dominating influence of Fola and Chiki and the eventual governorship of a university professor who is elected as the new state leader. Here, too, as in *Of Age*, Lamming uses creative art and culture as politically and pedagogically useful interventions in the dominance of colonial vision.

It is therefore ironic that the audience Lamming attempts to reach is still rather limited, a complaint that was even more serious in the fifties, when he first turned to writing novels. Lamming believes he was initially forced out of Barbados just as other Caribbean writers were forced to leave their own nations. He confronts this problem in "The Occasion for Speaking." Because readership was so curtailed in a largely illiterate and underappreciative society, writers in the Caribbean, he says, were "made to feel a sense of exile by our inadequacy and our irrelevance of function in a society whose past we can't alter and whose future is always beyond us" (24). A short while before Lamming himself was to leave for England in 1950, the West Indies were just emerging as a space of exceptional literary activity.[40] But in spite of the undoubted talent of the area, a lackluster public interest in West Indian fiction in the early thirties had driven several Caribbean writers away. Lamming mentions the seriousness of the problem, mitigated only by the support of local journals and magazines, on a number of occasions. In fact, he implies that Edgar Mittelholzer killed himself under conditions antagonistic to creative writing;[41] and upon C. L. R. James's death years later, Lamming declared that James was a "national treasure" who had never been adequately appreciated by his island of birth, Trinidad.[42] In posing the Caribbean so provocatively as a hostile space that literally causes "the death of the author," Lamming is not distancing himself politically from the Caribbean, although he says he was forced to do so physically. Rather, he blames colonial education for the anti-intellectual tradition of the islands. Most of the children, he says, were trained for examinations and tested for how much they could memorize.[43] In an atmosphere that developed little respect for what the indigenous cultures had to offer, Lamming seems to imply, it was hardly surprising that the work of novelists was largely ignored.

C. L. R. James, however, seems to have had little doubt about the value of the contributions from the archipelago. He said in an interview at the University of Texas as early as the seventies, "I do not know at the present time any country writing in English which is able to produce a trio of the literary capacity and effectiveness of Wilson Harris,

George Lamming, and Vidia Naipaul."[44] In the more recent *Culture and Imperialism*, Edward Said extends the accolade to James, marking his intellectual influence on writers like Lamming and situating both of them as key figures in the transition from colonialism to decolonization. In spite of Lamming's bleak perception of indifferent audience receptiveness, his works and those of other writers of his generation belonged, according to Said, to an important body of "resistance culture." Said goes on to yoke anticolonial resistance in the Caribbean to a "cultural effort" that arose "in India; in German, French, Belgian, and British Africa; in Haiti, Madagascar, North Africa, Burma, the Philippines, Egypt, and elsewhere," in a global network that had an impact on issues ranging from literary expressions to national statehood. And even if the relevance of the former to the latter may not have been immediately apparent, the voices of postimperial writers in these parts of the world, Said rightly claims, "are not only an integral part of a political movement, but in many ways the movement's *successfully* guiding imagination, intellectual and figurative energy reseeing and rethinking the terrain common to whites and non-whites."[45]

Nevertheless, Lamming's complaint about the lack of an audience is put in perspective by his role at Rodney's funeral. Some of the WPA members, students at the University of Guyana, clearly approved of Lamming's oratory but confessed that they had not read his novels. "They too hard," they said. "All them chaps too hard, Lamming, Wilson Harris, Walcott."[46] Lamming himself is aware of his departures from the usual traditions of novelistic fiction with which most of us trained in such conventions were familiar before postcolonial and postmodern reading strategies forced us to unlearn some things and relearn others.[47] Of his narrative strategies, Lamming says, "There is often no discernible plot, no coherent line of events with a clear, causal connection. Nor is there a central individual consciousness where we focus attention, and through which we can be guided reliably by a logical succession of events" (*Castle*, xxxvi). His prose style sometimes approaches the thoughts of Marcia, one of his characters in *Of Age:*

> Words were collecting in her head, vague and vagrant like a movement of shadows over an indifferent surface. She could almost feel them stray, as though they refused to obey their normal use. They slipped from their meaning, sailing briefly like feeble noises that stumble for a while before returning to the silence which contains them. The signs did not cohere.[48]

So while the students' diffidence is not entirely difficult to comprehend, my concern here is for the apparent resolution of the problem.
Noting this episode at the funeral, the Guyanese intellectual Andaiye
turned ultimately to the accessibility of Lamming's public speeches.
Here, in the divide between the written text and the oral performance
lies the double bind in Lamming's formulation about West Indian literature and its peasant inspiration. And here, too, lies the disjunction
between the oral practices embodied in the Vodoun Ceremony of the
Souls and the novelist's appropriation of the role of the *houngan*, the
priest-mediator.

If Lamming's written work is perceived as inaccessible not simply
through lack of publishing outlets and critical feedback, but because his
work is too "hard" for students within the institutional site, what does
this say about his apparent subjects, the peasants themselves, assuming
that they might also find the formal prose of a nineteenth-century
British genre alienating, however adapted to twentieth-century
Caribbean folk culture and oral expression? One could very well suggest that they might, like the students, prefer his oral performance, but
this ignores Lamming's formulation on the ascendancy of the novel. At
one point in "Occasion," impatient with apologists for West Indians
writing in English, Lamming understandably says, "I am not much
interested in what the West Indian writer has brought to the English
language. . . . A more important consideration is what the West Indian
novelist has brought to the West Indies" (36). Let us extend the question in the light of Lamming's stated concern for peasant life and ask:
"What has the West Indian writer brought to peasant culture?" We
already know Lamming's answer: the attention to the significance of
"these lives—the world of men and women down below" (*Castle*,
xxxvii). Accepting this for the moment, let us move to other questions
raised by Lamming's formulation, made, we must remember, within
the general context of defending the significance of West Indian writing
in a society that ignores its contributions.

Many of the issues regarding the relevance of writing for largely
illiterate groups or among audiences not trained in the conventions of
the nineteenth-century traditions of the novel have already been
addressed by Ngũgĩ, who further muddies the waters by introducing
the problem of writing in English to a largely non-English-speaking
audience in Kenya.[49] Lamming, however, sweeps aside the issue of
choice of language. And as for doubts about the novel as an adequate
form, he insists that the novel in the Caribbean has been informed and

transformed by the peasant context. Hence he appropriates forms of collective memory from folklore and also invents his own myths, filtering them through his lower-class and rural characters, in order to articulate, through *his* peasant subject, resistance to European and colonial history, its antithetical other.

Although Dipesh Chakrabarty refers in the following passage to history and the peasants in India, his argument holds for theorizations of peasant subjects in Lamming's case as well:

> Thus peasant/worker constructions of "mythical" kingdoms and "mythical" pasts/futures find a place in texts designated . . . history precisely through a procedure that subordinates these narratives to the rules of evidence and to the secular, linear calendar that the writing of "history" must follow. The antihistorical, antimodern subject, therefore, cannot speak itself as "theory" within the knowledge procedures of the university even when these knowledge procedures acknowledge and "document" its existence. Much like Spivak's "subaltern" (or the anthropologist's peasant who can only have a quoted existence in a larger statement that belongs to the anthropologist alone), this subject can be spoken for and spoken of by the transition narrative that will always ultimately privilege the modern (i.e., "Europe").[50]

Chakrabarty does not intend to moralize against those who claim to represent the peasants, but rather urges the need to negotiate critically the compromised locus of institutional sites and disciplines. Because of our positions within these sites, he argues, third-world intellectuals are condemned to know Europe as the "original home" of the modern and to continue to address it even as we struggle to find ways out of the double bind.

To recognize Lamming's own position within the institutional sites of a largely middle-class domain is not, however, to reject entirely his metaphorical mantle of the *houngan*, who could also operate outside proletarian realms of practice. As my chapter on *Season* will demonstrate, Lamming assumes the status to express his commitment to writing about the lives of "the men and women down below" and about a past that had received little attention. But as in the case of his metaphorically presiding over the Ceremony of the Souls, Lamming's claims about fighting in the ranks of the peasants must similarly be distanced from a literal interpretation.[51] The novelist himself is unable to articulate any single "speaking subject" of history, to use Chakrabarty's phrase. The impossibility of tracing clear and rigid lineaments for the self/other dichotomy of the colonial paradigm is most clearly apparent in *Natives*, while Lamming's other novels experience the productive inability to compartmentalize private and public subjects. We can experience the subaltern only through Lamming's directing imagination, keeping in mind his claim that his imagination has been inspired most by peasant struggles around him. The means of communication between different sites of identity and practice make room for some exchange. In *Of Age* and *Season*, the radio functions as one such instrument of communication, although the author himself points out that it is controlled by the state. The place of the novel in the Caribbean, as Lamming was very well aware, is a far more vexed issue. Its effects on the middle class, which constitutes Lamming's general audience, are more available for study than its effects on the peasants, who remain Lamming's valued subjects. Chakrabarty's caution about not making general claims regarding either the textual subjects or the audiences on which they have an impact must temper any generalized assertions about the novel as a weapon of revolution. Lamming's revolutionary claims for the novel emerge from an anxiety about its overlooked potential in the Caribbean. Conversely, Ngũgĩ's claims for the revolutionary status of the novel, and later, theater, are located within a different set of conditions. Ngũgĩ argues that, ironically, the Gikuyu novel in the Kenyan context is censored by the state precisely because people pay too much attention to it.

In the conclusion, I return to the issues that introduce this project, moving from Lamming as a writer in the context of the fifties to the appropriateness of his work in the light of contemporary developments. Lamming himself seems to see little change in West Indian nations after independence, locating the United States as the new aggressor that replaced Britain. In the United States context that marks the production of this book, as long as Caribbean interests continue to be subsumed and aggregated within the program affiliations of Latin American *and* Caribbean Studies, indicating the academic ascendancy of the United States and the virtual disappearance of the Caribbean in what is largely a focus on Latin America in such programs, one cannot exaggerate the influence of literatures from the Caribbean. Nevertheless, a new interest in scholarship on the "black atlantic" relocates the Caribbean within emergent diaspora studies programs, though these, too, need careful articulation. Similarly, to return to Lamming's work within the Caribbean itself, the reconstructed discussions of hybridity and creolization in contemporary global and multicultural contexts have stimulated a consideration of the Caribbean as a postmodern, even futuristic, space that might set an example for racial and cultural combinations. Reading the Caribbean in too celebratory a global context, I argue, plays into its material touristification and ignores the continuities of colonialism that Lamming emphasizes while romanticizing the undoubted potential of its specific histories. Lamming's own return to the Caribbean after decades in exile resituates his emphasis on the Caribbean as a provisional base for the migrant intellectual who now operates in a centripetal rather than a centrifugal relationship to it.

In the conclusion I turn to calling up some "spirits" of my own, pointing to a significant absent presence in Lamming's energetic "conversations": the women writers.[52] In an interesting reversal in *Pleasures*, Lamming expands his first polemical claim of being Caliban's descendant. He is also Prospero's "direct descendant," he amends, and uses his language "not to curse our meeting—but to push it further" in a future that "must always remain open" (15). While this desire to move beyond binaries and continual recrimination is commendable, what Lamming does not take into account in this essay is what Sylvia Wynter calls "the non-desire of Caliban for his own mate." [53] The tropological triad of Shakespeare's three prominent characters in *The Tempest* extends only to Miranda, a white woman. Lamming's discussion of women's issues in *Natives* is sensitive to their exclusion but ends with the conversation between white female characters. Here, too, black women remain silent, although they are a strong presence in some of his other novels. But Lamming himself would admit that they can no longer be ignored and, indeed, *must* no longer be ignored. The Lady implies in *Natives* that the men's behavior to the women will lead to their undoing, and in some ways, she is right. As the women confront their status in the New World, they discover "the same sound of absence," and the "same smell of absence" as at home. But the last page of the novel, it turns out, has the last word only insofar as it can predict an uncertain future, a future that, given the devastation of the events we have witnessed, contains only a hint of promise.

Part 1. Voyages

Chapter 1

Allegory, Parody, and Alterity in *Natives of My Person*

> We also, of our princely grace, for us, our heirs and successors,
> will, straightly charge, make and ordain that the said province be
> of our allegiance, and that all and every subject and liege people
> of us, our heirs and successors, brought or to be brought, and
> their children, whether there born, or afterwards to be born,
> become natives and subjects of us, our heirs and successors, *and
> be as free as they who were born in England.*
> —From the charter granting ownership of Barbados "and many
> other islands" to the Earl of Carlisle by Charles I

In an apparently excessive move, in the essay "Occasion for Speaking,"
George Lamming places on the West Indian novel the same historical
weight that he gives Columbus's entry into the so-called New World
and the ending of slavery centuries later.[1] While the relationship
between what has since been recognized as the initiation of a unique
period in world history and the local emergence of a genre might at
first seem baffling, it is precisely the role of writing in the process of recognizing the momentous consequences of Columbus's "error" that
makes Lamming's emphasis on the novel understandable. Richard
Helgerson directs attention to a fundamental catalyst in the colonizing
venture: "Everyone knows what Columbus did in 1492, but not everyone remembers what he did in 1493. He wrote an account of his voyage
and made it available for publication." The production of the text following hot upon the heels of the event vindicates Lamming's shrewd
categorization of the act of writing as a historical event in itself. As Helgerson goes on to argue, "the single, most important feedback mechanism . . . and the most important body of self-representations of Euro-

peans in the act of encountering and exploiting those distant regions was the printed voyage."[2] Clearly, historiography was just as instrumental as literature in setting the mechanism in motion. But while Columbus's text and the scores that followed complemented the imperial voyages that were to shape the modern Caribbean, Lamming chooses the West Indian novel as a historical event that attempts to expose and repair the scars of that arrival.

Columbus's entry into the Caribbean five hundred years ago, followed by ever-increasing European expansion, set the stage for a historically distinct and substantial body of work related to the economy of travel, trade, and their later offshoot, tourism. But the colonial discourse of Eurocentric travel narratives valorized the voyages, migrations, and settlements as euphoric occasions illustrating the courage of the explorers and adventurers. Lamming therefore locates the West Indian novel in opposition to the performance of arrival as well as to the celebratory nature of the chronicles that record it. While the novel may seem too broad a category of oppositionality, he includes the entire genre in order to assert that not just a particular group of novels, but the genre itself provided the most productive space to engage, directly or indirectly, the issues raised by colonialism.

The literary endeavors that represented the epic grandeur of colonizing ventures through the late sixteenth and mid–seventeenth centuries invigorated European political and economic expansion. The production of the European as a universal agent with a legitimate history corresponded, albeit inversely, with the construction of what lay outside the boundary of European space and subject position as either a cultural chaos requiring control or as a material paradise demanding settlement. The either/or construction here is perhaps deceptive since, as Peter Hulme argues, the discourse of the savage dissimulated the discourse of land:[3] both discursive configurations of the New World contributed to the justification and establishment of colonial settlement. To assert the nonhumanity of the peoples encountered during the voyages or even to claim not to see them; to frame what amounted to armed invasion and aggressive and exploitative trade practices in the language of discovery, civilization, and enlightenment; to ascribe a lack of history, culture, and agency to the so-called Amerindians and Africans—these were ideological activities essential to the material practice of empire. According to such ideologies, the history of the "discovered" nations began with the advent of colonial rule.

For the Caribbean, in particular, repopulating the islands for the purpose of plantation labor brought into intimate but violent contact the peoples of the Americas, Europe, Africa, and Asia. Lamming's sixth novel, *Natives of My Person,* inserts itself directly into the triumphal discourse of early slaving and settlement enterprises that followed mercantile capitalism. Redeploying the primary phase of colonization, circumnavigation,[4] and tracking the adventures of familiar characters in travel accounts, the novel presents a composite jumble of narratives by the Commandant, Boatswain, Priest, the Lady, and other allegorical figures. Through the archaic prose and overblown rhetoric of these accounts, Lamming parodies the ideological assumptions behind such adventures and turns on their head the largely unself-conscious racism and bigotry of the European narratives. Told in three sections, "Breaking Loose," "The Middle Passage," and "The Women," *Natives* describes a colonial adventure that goes awry.

If, as Benedict Anderson argues, print-as-commodity made the "horizontal-secular, transverse-time" of nationalism possible,[5] then the spatial cartographies of each nation were mapped by the sweep of capital in search of new markets. Marx provides us with an inside view of what was going on in England before and during the supposedly ennobling voyages, revealing the ugly reality of "the secret of primitive accumulation." The massive transformations that he outlines suture the bloody and violent history of expropriation in England with exploitation in the colonies, both of which nourished the process of capitalist accumulation. Large masses of peasants were torn from their land in England and forced to sell their labor to the landed owners of the means of production. To the creation of the European global subject that Mary Louise Pratt describes,[6] Marx would add a vital ingredient: the formation of "one great market provided for by industrial capital." The unfolding horror story, deliberately puncturing the assertions of a glorious period of empire, extends outside Europe as the landed proprietors and merchants, in their incessant search for land and money, throw their nets over the incipient colonies. Marx summarizes:

> The discovery of gold and silver in America, the extirpation, enslavement and entombment in mines of the indigenous population of that continent, the beginnings of the conquest and plunder of India, and the conversion of Africa into a preserve for the commercial hunting of blackskins, are all things which characterize the

dawn of the era of capitalist production. These idyllic proceedings
are the chief moments of primitive accumulation.[7]

The ironic tone of the last line challenges the triumphant flourish of a
history Marx uncovers as an ugly and brutal one. The domestic labor
scene in England, in particular, was accompanied by the violently
inflicted international division of labor. The double narratives were
intermeshed: many members of the landless proletariat in England
were transformed into "beggars, robbers, and vagabonds" who would
eventually join the colonial enterprise, particularly when the circumstances of capitalist accumulation at home forced many of them to seek
redress elsewhere, often at the expense of others.

Masking the effects of such procedures, the imperialist account of
colonial voyages constructed energizing myths that presented the
adventurers as heroic, larger-than-life figures, and reduced the natives
to insignificant, even invisible objects. Using the familiar trope of the
ship at sea, Lamming addresses this "total blindness," the inevitably
flawed vision of imperialism, through the imaginative and parodic representation of one of the the initial voyages that would eventually lead
to the historic settlement of the islands. The planned journey of the
aptly named ship, the *Reconnaissance*, from the Kingdom of Lime Stone
to the Isles of the Black Rock, or San Cristobal, to build a colony there is
patterned on the historical journals and logs depicting the "pacifica-
tion" of the Caribbean.

Stephen Slemon identifies colonial discourse as the "pretext" of
postcolonial literary and historical writing, a structure that explains the
allegorical nature of Lamming's response in his novel. "Allegory, that
is, becomes an historically produced field of representation upon
which certain forms of postcolonial writing engage head-on with the
interpellative and tropological strategies of colonialism's most visible
figurative technology," Slemon argues.[8] However, he carefully distin-
guishes between varieties of allegorical responses. Unlike Fredric Jameson, who reads "all third-world texts" as "national allegories,"[9] Slemon
draws attention to particular texts that use allegory as a distinct tech-
nique rather than as a national mode of representation. In his opinion,
postcolonial allegories are direct responses to the codes already embedded in imperialist discourse and practice. Colonialist discourse, for
instance, interprets, identifies, or names people, places, and events with
reference to an anterior set of signs located in what is familiar to the

dominant cultures. Meanings attached to new and exotic "texts" have less to do with the specific historical and cultural contexts of the latter than with the predetermined lexical and semantic fields available to the colonizers. Hence the allegorical matrix is already available in imperialist discourse—in the discourse of the Old and the New Worlds. Postcolonial allegories appropriate the dual system of interpretation that underlies the production of imperialist history in order to dismantle the master code. Slemon acknowledges the problem of "post-colonial literary activity [being] overshadowed by a discourse of Empire," but argues that this discourse will first have to be usurped and unsettled if structures of power that have invented and facilitated this discourse are to be transformed.[10] This is precisely Lamming's project in the novel.

In traversing already traveled spaces with the purpose of defamiliarizing the familiar, *Natives* challenges and subverts both the literary and historical authority of travel narratives and the conditions that supported their production. But it expects readers to be conscious of the rhetorical strategies of the "Old World" and the "New World" and the various subtexts and pretexts that underwrite a parodic allegory. In spite of his use of pastiche, Lamming's purpose in addressing previous modes of recognition is to question the validity of authorship and authority and not simply to reproduce them. Since dominant versions of history institutionalize a particular perception of the past, a perspective that is based on the premises of allegory—no possibility of direct signification, no straightforward relationship between text and event, no stable objective reality, and no final closure—punctures the claims to truth and knowledge made by such versions. Through the juxtaposition of various narratives and voices, the novelist invites readers to note the discrepancies in varieties of perceptions and to participate in the process of critical revision enabled by the allegorical layering.

By its very nature, therefore, allegory distances itself from the original truth and exposes its illusory nature even as it unsettles the original. *Natives* begins with a reference to "the lawful history of those trading adventures which had brought such wealth and power to the Kingdom of Lime Stone."[11] But it proceeds, in its fictional reenactment of one such adventure, to inscribe its own texts on "the lawful history," thus providing an unstable series of accounts that open up the original to ironic reversal. The framework of the quest or voyage is a typical structure of traditional allegories. The narrative action occurs at the level of a journey, allowing allegory to move beyond a static representation of abstract ideas. The kinetic drive of allegory is expressed through the change and process available at the literal or structural level, and the growth and learning possible at the metaphorical one. The usually credible, but fallible, hero undertakes a journey that opens up the possibility of transformation in both the character(s) and the audience. The predictable contingencies of the journey work to transform the hero at a spiritual level, as in the case of the chivalric quest.[12]

A similar, albeit material, process of conversion informs the structure of travel narratives and adventure tales during the period of colonial settlement. In these works a series of events in a remote and usually threatening setting develop the skills and virtues of the central character(s). In a traditional travel/adventure narrative, the challenges encountered in journeying into unknown lands involve the formation of an individual heroic character that eventually has its effects on the larger community to which he—I use this pronoun deliberately—belongs. Although women actively participate in the process, usually their main course of entry is to follow the path set by their male counterparts, often to reproduce the community in the elsewhere of the nation. The effect of such narratives on the national character cannot be underestimated, since the heroes of these narratives are largely asserted as agents of civilization and their own national culture. The imperial quest is believed to improve the sensibilities of both the conquering heroes and the conquered natives, who are supposed to have the benefit of the edifying potential of the metropolis. England's tremendous maritime power, for example, allowed Britannia to rule more than the waves; it transplanted its nation space to distant lands even as it enriched itself in the reverse process. As Anderson would say, the "short, tight, skin of the nation [is stretched] over the gigantic body of the empire."[13]

Natives begins with a presentation of the "noble" ambitions of various adventurers, especially the officers, who are contrasted with the coarser crewmen, but in an ironic manner, as the narrative makes clear in the events that follow. Even before he sails for the Isles, the Commandant writes in his diary:

> *I declare it was my pride and no less to build from this battalion of van-*
> *dals and honest men alike such an order as might be the pride and exam-*

ple for excellence to Lime Stone herself; that I would plant some portion of
the Kingdom in a soil that is new and freely chosen, namely the Isles of the
Black Rock, more recently known as San Cristobal. For I have seen men of
the basest natures erect themselves into gentlemen of honor the moment
they were given orders to seize command over the savage tribes of the
Indies. Here is a perfect school in the arts of conquest and command!
(10–11, emphasis in original)

The idealism, sense of adventure and hope, and the explicit faith in
heroic transformation are expressed at the expense of the "savage
tribes," who are facilitators and objects of the art of conquest. In fact,
the very act of conversion must be accomplished through the conquered bodies of the tribes. They, along with their lands and resources,
are the raw materials in the pedagogy of "conquest and command."
The Tribes in the novel, one of the challenges to be overcome in the
journey, are consequently shown to be diminished by the adventurers,
who correspondingly increase in stature. In a parallel move, the
exploitation of the colonized peripheries, supposedly "new and freely
chosen," enables the growth and advancement of the core countries.
But just as this exploitation is justified by myths of development and
free will, the domination of the Tribes is disguised by philanthropic
motives. Surgeon plans to set up a hospital on the Isles; Steward
intends to build an orphanage. Neither openly acknowledges the private ambitions and fears that drive the officers away from the Kingdom
in search of a new life.

All the officers in the novel are identified allegorically through
their functions, the depersonalization suggesting their instrumentality
as social and institutional markers and also satirizing their own disregard for the specific histories of those over whom they seek mastery.
The functional signifiers of the names undercut the power of nomina-
tion and description that the voyagers will exercise over the natives
and the land. Although the voyagers themselves believe they are
unique, what such common names indicate is the banality and mass
production of their voyages. Similarly, the diaries, extracts, logs, and
maps generated by the journey provide the narrative structure that will
ultimately come undone. Diaries, in particular, recur in Lamming's
novels as a narrative strategy and a tropological site for the public revelation of personal secrets, but they offer personal perspectives that
cannot always be trusted. Nor can one always claim to know what is

going on in the texts based on the dense, interrupted, and convoluted composition of the plot. Ultimately, the narrative framework of *Natives* renders suspect the assertions of knowledge, coherence, and control inscribed in navigational aids such as diaries and maps.

The signifying practice of making notes and drawing maps provides ample opportunity for parody, as Lamming shows. The unabashed racism that underwrote the social, geographic, scientific, physiological, psychological, and philosophical contours of native identity and foreign landscape belied the truth-telling claims of the narratives. Further warping an already distorted history starkly exposes the ludicrous in what is held up to scrutiny.[14] Subject to the equally ruthless disorienting strategies of plot, language, and point of view, the readers of *Natives* are violently forced to confront the impossibly indeterminate status of truth and lie. Lamming's point, however, is not to assert blandly that all history is subjective, but to expose the consequences of power run amok in the camouflage of adventure.

In partnership with naming and cataloging, maps also constructed a particular vision of the Europeans as intrepid voyagers and hardy settlers and the non-Europeans as backward natives and brute savages. Ligon's map of Barbados, along with his "true and exact history" of Barbados, unself-consciously reveals that vision in the iconic depiction of people, settlement areas (with English names), and the clearly dominating presence of armed Europeans on horseback, engaged in chasing a pair of unarmed men fleeing on foot.[15] Of course, those same symbols inscribed in the visually captive and corraled territory allow a different interpretation to which Lamming turns: conquest involves the mutual degradation of both sides.

The maps in *Natives* portray a similar and literal marginalization of slaves, Amerindians, and landscape as items of profit for the voyagers. Throughout, the battle for the maps by the Commandant emblematizes the struggle for control and direction. The daily logs of the sailors form other conventional and commonsensical items of information and explication, overshadowed by the Commandant's own narrative. The sailors, for instance, are fascinated by the Commandant's obsession with writing and are aware that this art/act is connected to navigating both his journey and its account: "this vision of ink, large and inescapable as the coast, making black rivers everywhere, increasing the mysterious power of the word on paper" (133).

But even as the control of the word is asserted, Lamming's own narrative tactics unwind the tightly knit cohesion of these master narratives. The series of italicized notes in fine print on Steward's map is made to reveal its economic imperative, which, in turn, exposes the dehumanization and arrogance embedded in the language: *"Town is docile, safe, and plentiful in foods. Nuts and spice a common delicacy ten miles inland. Perfect for watering and fresh provision. Inhabitants will war if there be cause, but have no heart for victory. A good traffic in black cargoes"* (92). The notes constantly interrupt the conversation between Steward and Boatswain as the latter describes the mass suicide of the Tribes at Sans Souci, and they also follow a passage that praises the "industry" and "passion for learning" that Steward displays. The recurring interruptions in the form of these notes, visually and conceptually set off from the main narrative, ironically gloss the map and the oral account of victory that, in Steward's view, legitimates his knowledge and power. The notes, then, function as dryly rendered voice-overs that distract our attention from the dialogue between the characters. In not substituting for the dialogue but instead commenting on it, the notes set up a dialogue of their own with the readers, adding to the already deliberately thickened narration.

The reduction of the natives and the terrain into profitable marginalia that directs the course of the voyage epitomizes the ontological status and material appropriation of the "other" people encountered by the Europeans. But the constitutive acts of naming and mapping are largely illusory, as Peter Hulme reminds us in *Colonial Encounters*. In a detailed analysis of the discursive morphology of the word *canibal*, its subsequent attachment to the term *Carib*, and its encoding within the descriptive ideology of cannibalism, in the common stereotypes of the fierce Carib versus the gentle Arawak, Hulme argues that archival materials prove to be deceptive sources. The dubious history and anthropology that Hulme uncovers and the lack of what he calls "ethnic self-ascription" make it virtually impossible to read back in any verifiable manner the histories of the Amerindians.[16] As Hulme points out, the category of the Caribbean is itself a European invention. None of the names or descriptions is transparent; their cloudiness is aggravated by the fact that much of the world knew of the Amerinidians only *after* the contact with the Europeans, a contact that almost annihilated the former. The fact that the natives of these islands were called "Indians" as a result of an error that would have been comic had it not been for its terrible consequences, is in itself a statement of the misapprehension of these people. In spite of all those prolific eyewitness accounts and all the learned scholarship, Hulme convincingly argues, very little that is concrete is known about them.

Lamming allegorizes this lack of knowledge, this peculiar blindness of colonial vision, by making the Tribes themselves invisible in the text. There is no visual presentation of them, only indirect accounts. Their own presence is marginal, as they hover in the background, just beyond the direct vision of the invaders. In staying largely out of sight, an unknown and shadowy presence beyond surveillance and control, they symbolize the deepest fears of the colonizers, whose anxiety about the possibility of insurrections lead them to suppress the native populations in increasingly brutal ways. The identity and strength of the settlers depend on their rigid separation from the natives and on a denial of shared humanity. For Lamming, however, the Tribes function as more than a symbol of the invaders' blindness and paranoia. In a powerful reversal, the blindness of the sailors is their critical weakness, and the invisibility of the Tribes, the latter's most effective weapon. The narrow and blinding orbit of power and the limited foresight of the Commandant and his company lead to a bitter defeat at the hands of the Tribes, who remain tantalizingly near and yet unseen. Narrative control over their activities is rendered futile, and the self-proclaimed knowledge of the voyagers proves insufficient as their foolhardiness is punished.

Attempts to fix the Tribes physically in space also fail as the natives themselves dodge the more visible travelers, their mobile bodies using what is to them a familiar landscape to make proximity difficult. In depicting the presence of the native body as unconfirmed, Lamming explodes the boundaries of the metaphor of invisibility: the natives were indeed forced to "disappear." Amerindians frequently stole back to the islands in the darkness of the night, crept into the woods, and left the islands under cover of leafy disguises. In *Natives* and in Lamming's earlier novel, *Of Age and Innocence,* the landscape functions as a strategic weapon for the surviving Tribes, although they die in large numbers at the hands of the armed invaders, called the "Bandit Kings" in *Of Age.* Their genocide marks another kind of disappearance, a permanent one, bringing out the bitter pathos of Lamming's attempt to commemorate their history.

The lack of ocular proof and the vanished traces of Amerindian bodies also reflect ironically on the complacent fixity of settlement records and illustrated maps. The forcible inscription of new signs of human presence erase or alter the old ones, the negation of the latter allowing the expansion of the former. Barbados itself was said to be uninhabited when the first British colony was established in 1627. Although San Cristobal in *Natives* and other novels is a composite West Indian island, I will seek parallels primarily with Barbados, partly because of Lamming's national status and partly because the allegorical name for San Cristobal in *Natives* is the Isles of the Black Rock, perhaps coming from the series of black rocks outlining the coast of Barbados in maps such as Ligon's.

Although Portuguese and Spanish traders and colonists had sighted Barbados, whose name is derived from Portuguese, before the British, they had not established a settlement there, but they did succeed in driving off the Amerindians. When captain John Powell, the elder, landed on the island in 1625, he took possession of it in the name of James I, then King of England, just as sailors from Sir Olive Leigh's vessel had claimed it in 1605. The subsequent struggle for possession of the island demonstrates how appropriate its history was for the parody to which Lamming subjects it in his novel. The various sightings, "discoveries," and claims over islands that appear in the texts of the voyagers are impelled by a frenzied desire to grab as much land as possible before other competing European powers staked claim to it. The game of colonial monopoly was, of course, played with a merry disregard for the rights of those already inhabiting the land. In fact, they were included as part of the landscape as fit objects for servitude, enslavement, or removal. Portuguese, Spanish, French, and British documents portray the various and conflicting claims of possession that the representatives of each country made on behalf of their respective God, be he Catholic or Protestant, and their particular monarch, male or female. In 1626, Barbados was given "exclusively" to the French Sieurs d'Enambuc and du Rossey, on the grounds that they were "to spread the Catholic Faith and to establish as much trade and commerce as possible . . . considering that the inhabitants of the islands are not friendly people. . . ."[17] In 1627, soon after the Powell settlement, Charles I granted the charter making Barbados and neighboring islands, "as yet void and inhabited, in some places, with savages, who have no knowledge of the divine power," the property of James Hay, the first Earl of Carlisle.[18] In one casual sweep, the majestic generosity of the sovereign delivered islands and inhabitants into the hands of a man who was to be an absentee and largely indifferent proprietor.

But that was not all. In the temporary absence of the Earl of Carlisle, Charles I was prevailed upon by the Earl of Pembroke to take into consideration the primary right that Sir William Courteen had to the island, since John Powell had been financed by him. According to one interpretation, the king had first granted the royal patent to Courteen but seemed to have revoked it, through either forgetfulness, whimsy, or anger at the peer. Pressed by the Earl of Pembroke, he gave the island to Courteen until Carlisle returned and complained, forcing the harried king to restore the island to Carlisle. My point in detailing this anecdote is to illustrate the considerable contempt for island and inhabitants shown in the way the land is royally signed off with such beatific insouciance. Some of these patents and grants even included nonexistent islands. Wrenching these grand documents from those who wielded their pen with careless power, Lamming challenges their assumption of divine authority and feudal obligation.

The discourse of divinity played an important but conflictual role in the sanctioned authority of possession, as the language of royal decrees on land ownership makes clear. Paradoxically, both savage and God are made other than human, one losing power and the other gaining it as a consequence. "God and the cannibal, equally elusive, are assigned by the text the role of the Word in whose name its writing takes place—but also the role of a place constantly altered by the inaccessible (t)exterior [hors-texte] which authorizes that writing," says de Certeau.[19] The invaders' Christian identity ordains the enslavement of the natives, whose captivity is hallowed through their introduction to the right religion. Given the glorification of suffering in Christian mythology and the disavowal of material wealth, slaves could be ideologically controlled through sermons preaching endurance and unworldliness. Meanwhile, the Protestant ethic of hard work and individual enterprise aided the settlers in establishing plantations.

In Natives, Priest intends to save heathen souls in an act of violence that is expected to cleanse and redeem them. "His faith fell like an axe on the innocent flesh of the infidels," says the unnamed narrator, a recurring figure in Lamming's novels (111). Priest dispatches vast numbers of the "infidels" into slavery, convinced that "conversion through ownership" is a justified strategy of ensuring the liberation of souls through the bondage of bodies. The satirized appropriateness of the image of this born-again Priest "carrying the Gospel like a sword" becomes evident in the actual annihilation of the Tribes and the slaves in the process of their conversion.

The contradictions in religious participation in the slave trade were many. All human beings were capable of salvation if coerced or coaxed into the right religion, but dark skinned slaves were never quite assigned the status of human beings. Indeed, in the Renaissance allegories of Christianity, as racial divisions began to take on the colors with which we are now familiar, blackness was not just the antithesis of good, but seemed a natural accompaniment to beastliness as well. The detailed descriptions of the unloading of animals at the pier in *Of Age and Innocence* recall a similar disembarkment during the slave trade, except that those forced ashore and dragged in for inspection were human beings.

On the secular side, the enslavement of the natives was justified through the rhetoric of civilization and culture. The Commandant in *Natives* reflects with some anger on the "animal perseverance" of the Tribes (implicitly dispelling the myth of easy conquests and worshipping natives). In the face of his endorsed invasion, their refusal to submit seems irrational. "But resistance was a liberty he could not allow. He would never understand their cannibal refusal to surrender; servitude could hardly be a punishment in their animal state . . . it was lunacy to desecrate such gifts [language, civilization, etc.] with an open insult," says the narrator, presenting the Commandant's thoughts (65). The perception of an absence of humanity in the natives is an absolute factor that reads every act of theirs, whether submission or resistance, in terms of this absence. Further, it reinforces their invisibility at the symbolic and literal levels. The Tribes of San Cristobal who remain uncaptured literally disappear from the vision of the invaders, pushed further and further back into the margins as the superior firepower of the invaders makes direct confrontation difficult.

bell hooks locates the margins, traditionally positions of powerlessness, as productive sites of vision and knowledge. "Living as we did—on the edge—we developed a particular way of seeing reality. We looked both from the outside in and from the inside out. We focused our attention on the center as well as on the margin. We understood both."[20] Lamming is also interested in a way of seeing that disrupts center-focused colonial vision. In his interview with George Kent, the novelist points out that it is false to assume that only the colonized have had to confront the trauma of colonialism and that those in the center have been unmoved by the process. "The colonial experience is not just the experience of colonized people, but a very deep psychic experience of the colonizer himself. And the colonizer is imprisoned in that experience no less than the colonized," he says. The journey cuts both ways: the imperialists have also been degraded by their participation, though it would seem as if they were the victors. As Lamming suggests to Kent, "The Europeans had a middle passage, too, one that is now going to be seen on the interior of their lives." He continues in an address to an imaginary voyager: "I see you think that was a glorious moment; now let me show you how that moment was being seen from the other side."[21]

The "glorious moment" Lamming refers to is the celebration of the imperial conquests as in Hakluyt's *Voyages*, a text that he claims in the interview had a direct influence on the novel. Richard Hakluyt, a "preacher and sometime student of Christ-Church in Oxford," as the title page announces, published, between 1598 and 1600, three volumes of *The Principal Navigations, Voyages, Traffiques, and Discoveries of the English Nation*,[22] an anthology of letters, diaries, logs, and official correspondence of English sailors that soon became a trusted handbook of merchants, explorers, seamen, and geographers. The editor of the *Portable Voyages*, Irwin R. Blacker, has this to say of the monumental work: "The collection is Elizabethan in its vitality and scope, with all the greatness attributable to that age; at the same time it is more—in its panorama of the revealed birth of an empire and the opening of the globe, the *Voyages* has no equivalent in the English language."[23] Blacker also attests to the generic flexibility of such a collection, implying that travel literature served many uses. He suggests reading it as papers of empire, as accounts of trade, as geographical information, as political propaganda, as historical document, as personal narrative, as navigational material, and finally, as epic literature, supplementing each disciplinary and generic possibility with an explanation. As a result of their scope, Hakluyt's volumes had a profound influence. When Hakluyt was gathering sources for his first volume, England, as Blacker notes, played a minor role in international politics. By the time Hakluyt published his last volume, the small and parochial nation had been transformed into a major maritime power and a flourishing empire, defining its identity both within the nation and outside of it.

Lamming would agree that the *Voyages* was indeed a text of empire, although he would not use Blacker's laudatory tone in stating its fundamental importance. The collection includes, among other narratives, several eyewitness accounts of voyagers who were engaged in trade and slavery along the coastline of Africa and in the East and West Indies. Trade, however, was only the initial objective. A letter patent granted by Henry VII in the eleventh year of his reign to John Cabot, citizen of Venice, and his three sons charges them "to seeke out, discover, and finde whatsoever isles, countreys, regions or provinces of the heathen and infidels whatsoever they be." It goes on to authorize the Cabots to "subdue, occupy and possesse all such townes, cities, castles and isles of them found," and to require a share of the profit these activities would bring.[24] The various narratives justify and aggrandize the quest for power and glory with minimal consideration for the original inhabitants of the islands, who are identified typically by their "heathen" beliefs.

Lamming's use of the *Voyages* as an allegorical pretext in *Natives* comes through most clearly in his deployment of an extract from the former, an account of a voyage by Master Martin Frobisher in 1577. The typical navigational paradigms involving tempests, unfriendly natives, and hardships at sea are balanced by the praise of the seamen, who endure serious dangers for a "worthy" cause, and by the hope of saving the natives, "those barbarous people." But the natives of the island seem unappreciative of the noble intentions, as evidenced by the ferocious attack they launch on the intruders. So desperate are they to avoid being "saved" that the severely wounded leap off the rocks and drown themselves, while the survivors flee into the mountains. Frobisher marvels at these apparently illogical acts, coming to the conclusion that it is their lack of humanity and absence of finer qualities that motivate such folly.[25]

A similar episode is represented in the novel in Pierre's account of a slaving trip. In a reenactment of an earlier, symbolic episode in which masses of black seafowl descend on the ship and die in large numbers, the shackled slaves leap off the ship to their certain deaths, and like the seafowl, are consumed by the crocodiles (105). The seafowl innocently land on the ship and are then killed, an event that predicts the naivete of the natives, who, in another parallel account in Hakluyt by John Sparke, the younger, allow themselves to be fired upon by the voyagers. The narrator is blind to the analogous nature of these acts of violence, caused by the trust of the so-called savage creatures, and sees only their animal folly in both encounters.

As in the pretext of the *Voyages,* Pierre, echoing Frobisher's language, expresses amazement and horror at the mass suicide of the slaves, to him a *"great inconvenience"* and a clear sign of the *"absence of any soul"* and *"ignorance"* that are apparently a natural accompaniment to the *"blackness of hide"* (105, emphasis in original). The crocodiles themselves recall events recorded by the same John Sparke who delivers his "true" account of a voyage in the West Indies with Sir John Hawkins. Sparke describes the false tears of the crocodiles who beguile the unwary prey with their crying and snatch within their jaws those who venture too close. The crocodile incident in this account occurs just after Sparke condemns the parallel treachery of the Caribs, "eaters and devourers of any man they can catch, *as it was afterwards declared unto us* . . . ," who lure unsuspecting voyagers on to the island with offers of gold and then kill and allegedly eat them.[26]

In citing this passage, I have emphasized the last part of the quotation, so artfully and casually phrased, to recall Hulme's comments on how unreliable and secondhand "eyewitness" accounts can be. Sparke's subsequent comparison of the crocodiles with women who use tears to get their way with men is made without any understanding of the women's desperate recourse to what he considers contemptible tactics in the face of the more frank, upright strength of the manly invaders. Not only are women coyly deceitful, the natives, by implication, are made negatively effeminate against the macho forthrightness of the European mariners. Lamming, however, is attentive to the inequality of power and the resistance embodied in deceitfulness. In his text, the wily cunning of the Tribes, like that of the women and crocodiles reviled by Sparke, is a militant tactic and a strategy for self-defense rather than a flaw.

The attacks and suicides reported in the novel have their historical precedents in events during the Atlantic slave trade and settlement of the colonies. Suicide was common among slaves whose original social structures did not allow for the concept of bondage. Slaves from the Bight of Biafra were believed to be particularly unstable because they were unwilling to work on plantations and because large numbers of them died easily. Daniel Mannix records an "epidemic of suicide" among slaves who jumped overboard in spite of being chained together and, as a result, drowned almost immediately.[27] Counter-attacks and suicides belong to a long tradition of resistance that is mis-represented in colonialist versions. In the fixed code of colonial axiomatics, the invasion of the imperialists is represented as unique and heroic, while the actions of the natives and slaves are treacherous, irrational, and savage, indeed self-destructive. Rather than see these events as consequences of their brutality, the slavers preferred to attribute resistance to their maneuvers to the inhumanity and idiocy of those who struggled to escape them.

In *Natives*, the shortsightedness of absolute and arrogant power is repeated in the events that lead to the deaths of all the officers, each of whom is obsessed with being "an officer and a man on the inside." Their refusal to see what is on the outside results in the final violence onboard the ship and the disruption of their voyage. Pinteados, the Pilot and nonnative of Lime Stone who remains the outsider, sums up their weakness thus: "To be on the inside was enough. To be within the orbit of power was their total ambition" (319). Pinteados here refers not to the officers' relationship with the natives of the Isles, but to their interaction with the also unseen women on the sister ship accompany-ing the *Reconnaissance,* a vessel also allegorically named the *Penalty.* In the officers' privileging of the white male as the embodiment of humanity and bravery, as in Sparke's conflation of natives, women, and crocodiles, we see the dialectical interplay between the related sys-tems of racism and sexism. A sexualized vocabulary of conquest used by and about men, such as castration, impotence, rape, emasculation, and so on, tends to restrict resistance to the area of sexual politics alone, refusing violence and agency to women and reinforcing the structure of patriarchy.

Sexual metaphors of conquest operate extensively in the Comman-dant's language: *"men of the basest natures erect themselves into gentlemen of honor the moment they were given orders to seize command over the savage tribes of the Indies"* (11, emphasis in original). The kingdom on earth built through the implantation of "virgin territories" glorifies and rewards men of action, with the Tribes—both men and women—and the women of Lime Stone functioning as virgin guarantees of patriar-chal power. The images of hardness and virility associated with the Commandant illustrate the single-minded devotion to power that his name suggests. Yet, as Pinteados realizes, this inflexibility leads to his undoing and to the murder of the officers.

Allegorical traditions in colonialist literature portray the conquered continents as women who are reified into embodiments of a passive or threatening landscape that lay open to the masculine thrust of invasion. The polarized race and gender configurations operate within the Manichean mode of recognition. The unresisting white women and natives emerge as childlike, naive, and helpless, requiring the protection of the white male. The resistant, on the other hand, are depicted as deceitful, irrational, and sexually aberrant, calling for ruthless control. These binary oppositions in effect ignore native women, as many postcolonial feminists have pointed out, who are twice removed, in terms of race and gender, from the dominant center.

Lamming's perspective on native women emerges in relatively more detail in his earlier novels, *The Emigrants* and *Season of Adventure*. *Natives* deliberately restricts itself to the picture of the unindividuated, nameless mass of natives one sees in the *Voyages*, with only brief references to women and children. In the novel, the phallic metaphor of invasion is transferred from the women at home to the natives abroad. The Commandant perceives the Lady, like the land of San Cristobal, as one more area to explore and occupy. Lamming's use of the language of maritime exploration and conquest in describing the sexual relations between the two echoes the Commandant's vocabulary in the acquisition of land. The Lady herself makes the connection clear when, sensing the coming betrayal by the Commandant, she confronts him about the massacre of the Tribes and rejects the "Kingdom's triumphs" as acts of aggression and injustice. Her empathy for the Tribes, it must be remembered, is not exactly revolutionary, since it is expressed only after she realizes that the Commandant plans to leave her to attempt one more raid against the Tribes. Nevertheless, her painful insight troubles the Commandant, who reads her strength as a major flaw. "There's too much error in her virtue," he mourns (76).

Similar fears over their wives' "tyrannical virtue" drive Surgeon and Steward to goad their wives into doing something disastrous, and when this fails, they devise elaborate plans to humiliate the women. Impelled by a drive to dominate and unable to fulfill this drive satisfactorily with the women at home, the officers seek fresh areas in which to exercise their will to power. As Lamming puts it in his interview with Kent, "The corruption in the individual man/woman relationships between Steward and his wife, between Surgeon and his wife, and the difficulty between Boatswain and his woman—these are symptoms of a wider and more pervasive corruption of the society in which they lived."[28] The perverse manipulation within the home and nation is also carried outward into the colonies, to manifest itself in a different relational network.

The last section of the novel, entitled "The Women," a dramatic dialogue between the three wives, characteristically offers no solutions or neat closure but leaves both text and voyage inconclusive and ruptured. While the last line of the novel, "We are a future they must learn," suggests that the men cannot work productively with their current attitudes to women, the self-discovery of the women is undercut by their situation: they are left stranded on the island, unaware that the men they hope to share a future with have died a violent death some miles away (345). The fracture of the traditional idyllic tale of adventure reminds us that there can be no happy ending for a system that builds its utopia through oppressive practices. The violent conclusion of the officers' (mis)adventure also strategically reminds us of the high rates of mortality and failure in the establishment of colonies, although the dominant narrative is more likely to inscribe the enterprise as a success story. The deaths of the officers, however, do not signal freedom for the others. The blindness is sustained, not cured, by the failures of both the natives, whose infighting and internal oppressions make them easy targets, and the women, whose suffering has not, it seems, taught them much—they continue to wait and worship at the altar of the men.

In *The Pleasures of Exile,* Lamming aligns Miranda with Caliban in *The Tempest* as a figure defined and limited by Prospero's "magic," his control of her history, and her own inability to recognize the power of his rhetoric. "It is this innocence and credulity in Miranda which— were it not for a difference in their degrees of being—would have made her and Caliban almost identical," argues Lamming.[29] In a sense, both of them are caught up in Prospero's definition of who they are. Caliban is constituted as a threat to Miranda only when she is marked as a sexual being by Prospero because it is clear that there was a happier interaction between them before Caliban is accused of rape. The boundaries are then set up to maintain a separation between both of Prospero's subjects, a practice that was repeated when native males were perceived as a threat to white women. *Natives* ends with the women on the island and the Tribes hovering in the background, while the lower ranks of mutinous sailors, so despised by the officers, are also headed in the direction of the island. Whether this suggests a reorganization of the system or a continuation of exploitation is left unclear. What is striking about this convergence is that it brings together, in the final violence of the mutiny, the groups traditionally excluded in the hierarchy of colonial affiliation.

The intersections of class and gender come through in the Commandant's question, "Tell me, Steward . . . which do you really fear? Is it the woman? Or the men who are down below?" (177). Steward's evasive response is to assert that he can control the men, implying that upper-class women are a greater threat than lower-class men. The need to keep the men "down below" just where they are within the confines of the ship exemplifies the structure outside the ship's community, which merely replays what is on the mainland. The class boundaries between the ordinary seamen and the officers are clearly drawn, with the Commandant at the top of the hierarchy. His refusal to discuss his orders with the mariners reinforces the traditional structures of power through the restriction of knowledge. The idea of a forced union between the secret "cargo" of women and the sailors once they reach San Cristobal is stimulated by a fear of the coarse sexual appetite of the crew, which the Commandant constructs and then attempts to curb by the regulation of forced marriage. Both the nameless, hidden women on the sister ship who have been selected as mates and the general crew on the *Reconnaissance* are reified into objects of social and sexual control. We are told in Hakluyt's handbook that it was unlawful in 1588 to carry "any women or harlots" on board, although this may have been because the fleet in question was engaged in a military expedition against the Spanish Armada.[30] But the Commandant's decision to smuggle the women to San Cristobal and leave their presence undeclared also constructs them as illegal "cargo." The Commandant's rigid sense of class distinctions and his corresponding desire to dictate the behavior of the women is also revealed in his reaction to the knowledge that Boatswain and the Lady have had sexual relations. Though he is able to stomach her marriage to the corrupt Lord Treasurer, Gabriel Tate de Lysle, and even exploit it to commandeer the resources, including ships, for the secret journey, he finds her relationship with Boatswain intolerable, a reaction that moves him to suspend the voyage and face the threat of mutiny.

Mutiny, escape, and desertion by crews on the high seas during the period of slaving and settlement were common, especially before the strict patrolling by the Royal Navy in the eighteenth century. Common sailors were regarded as dregs of humanity and bore the brunt of the rigors of the voyages. Bad weather, lack of food and water, grueling work, hostile natives, sickness and death, cruel captains—this was the lot of the ordinary seaman of the period, realities that are sanitized in adventure narratives. Not surprisingly, the rate of mortality was very high. Some scholars argue that comparatively more seamen than slaves died during the horrific Middle Passage because the slaves were items of profit and were usually given preference when the rations ran short.[31] In stories about particularly vicious captains that present a mutated picture of the heroic adventurer, the differences in the torture inflicted on sailors and on slaves were of degree rather than kind.

The threat of insurrection was severe enough to be a major concern for both the merchants and peers who financed the enterprise and the officers who carried it out. The ordinances and instructions compiled by Sebastian Cabot in 1553 give primacy to the relationship between the officers and the crew:

> First the Captaine general, with the pilot major, the masters, marchants & other officers, to be so knit and accorded in unitie, love, conformitie, and obedience in every degree on all sides, that no dissention, variance, or contention may rise or spring betwixt them and the mariners of this companie, to the damage or hinderance of the voyage: for that dissention (by many experiences) hath overthrown many notable intended and likely enterprises and exploits.[32]

The rigorous enforcement of class distinctions as essential to the success of the voyage is particularly ironic since most of the voyages were seen as an escape from the oppressive class relations in the various home countries. Imperialism was presented as a corrective or outlet to social disorders in the core countries and the movement toward the peripheries was usually expressed through utopian ideals of building anew an egalitarian society. But in reality, the evolution of mercantile capitalism in the early phase of imperialism in England had a significant negative effect on the attitude toward poverty and unemployment, which began to be seen as consequences of vice and laziness. Even as the rich merchants began to assimilate into the aristocracy, the Tudor and Stuart governments became increasingly ruthless in suppressing revolts by landless peasants and artisans and by the growing number of unemployed in the cities. During Cromwell's reign, large numbers of rioters were shipped off to the West Indies to contribute to indentured labor on the island plantations. V. T. Harlow, quoting Thomas Carlyle in his *Life and Letters of Oliver Cromwell,* observes that the practice of shipping off recalcitrant political rebels and rioters became so common that it made an active verb of Barbados—to barbados someone meant to get rid of him or her in this manner.[33] Thus the movement out of the home country included in its trajectory the expansion of those in the center as well as the expulsion of those in the margins.

Lamming's inclusion of class and gender struggles within what is labeled as the core or the metropolis, which is then set in opposition to the periphery or the colony, reminds us that power relationships in a colonial framework did not operate through a simple binary, although generally speaking, the white male occupied a privileged position in the hierarchies of power. There were peripheries within the center and peripheries within the colony, the so-called periphery, toward which women, indentured laborers, and "poor whites" were pushed. It was not always a simple case of powerful white and oppressed black or privileged male and underprivileged female. The assymetrical relations of power were transferred to the colonies, as the Commandant's scheme shows.

Though the Kingdom of Lime Stone could represent any colonial power—the House of Trade and Justice, for instance, had its historical counterpart in Spain—its relationship to England can hardly be overlooked, given the British context of West Indian colonialism.[34] There are frequent references in *Natives* to a Northern revolt that seems to reflect the Northern and Western uprisings in England in 1569 and between 1626 and 1632, respectively. Political disorders on the domestic front were more common than conventional historiography would suggest in accounts of historical events and personalities in England. Contrary to official accounts of the uprisings, popular revolts were genuine and organized expressions of discontent.[35] An indication of widespread social problems is given in the Commandant's stern oratory to his squabbling crew, reminding them of the terrible conditions they would be forced to return to in the event of a failed voyage: "Of every age and sex you can see them plundering nature in the countryside. No sheep can trust the wool it wears when the Kingdom's army of vagabonds grows so large; men made barbarous and bitter by their hunger, eating rats and feeding off the very roots of plants not yet a day in the ground . . . From childhood to the grave there are men who have never known the ordinary smell of bread" (49).

In spite of his professed sensitivity to social problems, the Commandant tends to blame the greedy merchants for the country's decadence and to elevate his own aristocratic leadership of the sailors. At the critical moment, the Commandant is destroyed by his refusal to share power, and it is Baptiste, the powder maker with a long tradition of artisan resistance, who leads the sailors into mutiny and desertion. Significantly, Lamming names the ordinary seamen but refers to the officers only by their occupations, rejecting conventional paradigms by underlining the humanity of the crew. In a fiery speech to the sailors, Baptiste rejects the hierarchy both of the House of Trade and Justice and of the Commandant, and he urges the sailors to take control: "The same hands of authority organize your decay. They name you adventurers for the purpose of turning you into common animals of prey," he declares with an insight that comes, as in the case of the Lady, from an awareness of an interlocked series of consequences in the colonial expedition (306).

The traditional adventure narrative concludes with a safe arrival at the destined location or a happy return to the point of departure, with some gains made and several lessons learned. But Lamming's views on the inherent destructiveness of the imperial voyage are expressed in the final crisis and frustration of goals—the voyage is aborted and the birth of the empire is stalled. The suspension of the Commandant's plan draws attention to the nature of the transformation accomplished during an imperialist voyage. Unlike the Commandant, Lamming does not see the whole enterprise as enabling a development of sensibility and nobility, but rather as a dehumanizing, vicious labyrinth that traps both the colonizer and the colonized in endless cycles of violence. Like Aimé Césaire, he sees imperialism not as a glorious moment, but as a moral and spiritual crisis in European history. Césaire concludes with this thesis after making a series of claims that question the notion of heroism in any brutal exercise: "the colonizer, who in order to ease his conscience gets into the habit of seeing the other man as *an animal*, accustoms himself to treating him like an animal, and tends objectively to transform *himself* into an animal."[36]

Lamming challenges the claims of the inherent barbarism of the natives and the supposed civilization of the colonizers through his dramatization of Césaire's point. The title of the second section of the novel, "The Middle Passage," draws within its parameters both Europeans and non-Europeans, as Lamming indicates in his interview with Kent. The complicated use of the word *native*, melding the us and them, the familiar and unfamiliar, and the male and female, suggests the contradictions that surface when "persons" are objectified and nominally made other. Borrowing the phrase from a postcard in which an entire extended family is represented by an Ashanti man as "natives of my person," Lamming goes on to describe the aptness of the phrase for the characters in his novel and his own critical humanist relationship with his work and its social world, pictured through this metaphor of filiation.[37]

The cohesive and controlling global subject articulated in the persona of the adventurer is split by the competing lines of race, class, and gender, as well as by the gruesome history of the enterprise. The suspension of the carefully planned enterprise underscores the ultimate horror and futility of the colonial experience as the historical process overtakes and crushes the supposed controllers of history. In the confusion and anger of the mutiny, what we see is not an organizer of experience, but a fragmented and disrupted self embodied in Boatswain's attempts to claw and tear at his own flesh when his recollection of the Lady's treachery and the claustrophobic interior of the ship drive him insane. In *The Emigrants*, Lamming's account of West Indian emigration to England several hundred years after the colonizing voyages, the ship functions as a more comforting although still divided nation(s) space. The intimacies of life onboard help most of the immigrants to form a sense of comradeship in spite of national and individual differences. In *Natives*, however, although many of the mariners ultimately unite for the mutiny, the closed confines of the ship increase the tension and paranoia of the sailors. Rather than experiencing freedom from restraints in the search for adventure, they are made to feel on edge by the intransigent secrecy of the Commandant, who refuses on more than one occasion to let them go ashore.

The emblematic representations used throughout the novel suggest defeat and degradation on both sides, rather than glorious victory. The decaying corpse of the white sea hawk in the novel is an ominous symbol of the inevitable destruction of the enterprise, a "terrible omen of adventure." Lamming's graphic descriptions of fever and disease, of madness and cannibalism—among the voyagers rather than the Tribes—portray the rapid spread of decay and death, just as Steward's incest and Boatswain's delirium symbolize the predatory and self-destructive qualities of imperialism. The "plague of madness"—the "curse of the Black Coast," as Pinteados describes it—attacks the bodies of the sailors almost in revenge against the orderly inscriptions of the land through maps and print. The landscape may thus be contained, but it takes a severe toll, especially on those mariners who sail along the coast for "black flesh." Rather than describe the anguish of the slaves huddled in the hold, Lamming focuses instead on the self-inflicted wounds of the insane at Severn asylum: "But you didn't know what to do when the man was biting up his own tongue or tearing the skin from under his eyes. . . . In my time I hear many sounds, animal and otherwise in battle or sickness and dying; but nothing to compare with the human voice when it start to scream out from the cells at Severn" (159). In this passage, a foreshadowing of what is to happen to Priest, the mutilation of the tongue and eyes is particularly striking since the novelist damages the instrument of speech and the vision of those whose voice and sight he appropriates. Throughout the novel, in fact, the characters are constantly subject to blurred or watery vision.[38] Conditions in the interior of the asylum are made to parallel psychologically the tortured screams in darkened slave holds, the madness of the sailors a moral consequence of what Steward's wife calls "a power of blindness" (336), their refusal to see what was "down below" them.

The inflexible, dangerous environment, the tempests, and the unbearable heat described in the novel therefore operate, like the scene at Severn, "simultaneously as metaphor and metonymy," a characteristic of allegorical signification.[39] They are also historical realities. Hakluyt's *Voyages* records briefly the "continuall mortalitie" at sea as sickness and ague relentlessly strike the sailors and drive many of them insane. Malcolm Cowley presents in more detail a sober picture of what was involved in the reportedly triumphant adventure. Along with the deportation of millions of Africans and the deaths of a large percentage of them during the Middle Passage and the genocide of the native Indians, a "high proportion of the Europeans engaged in slaving died on the Guinea Coast of malaria, dysentery, acute alcoholism, or gunshot wounds, and most of the survivors were physically ruined or morally degraded beyond redemption."[40] The violence extended far beyond the actual passage, to the initial slaving raids, the wars among the natives, the attacks by pirates and adventurers, the intense rivalry between colonizing powers, and, finally, to the consequences of slavery and settlement in the colonies.

In his imaginative reconstruction of the colonizer's "Middle Passage," Lamming alludes to historical events even as he exposes the fictionality of much colonial history. Various scraps of narratives and events drift past the reader, dragging with them pieces of other narratives and events that are never fully clarified. The breakdowns in narrative and genre, the multiple perspectives that contradict rather than complete each other, and the complicated and profoundly ironic mirroring of early colonial history are all difficult areas to navigate. The difficulty of the text makes shaky and precarious the historical process of discovery and enlightenment as projected in colonial travel narratives. The master narrative is entangled in Lamming's reworking, and it emerges not as a univocal truth but as "a way of seeing" that is underwritten by a convoluted discourse and practice of power and knowledge. The Lady, for instance, slips in and out of the text through the points of view of the Commandant, Boatswain, and herself in a series of disconnected flashbacks that deconstruct each narrative revolving around her. Neither the Commandant nor Boatswain shares the same image of the Lady in their encounters with her, and her own account, which emerges most directly in the final section with the other women, challenges the perspectives of the male characters.

Lamming writes, on the surface, from the point of view of the early imperialist but he manipulates the deeper levels of meaning to bring the ironies of imperialist vision to the surface. The allegorical structure of *Natives* gestures in the direction of Hakluyt's *Voyages,* but parodies it to reveal the bias and bombast of the latter. In a sustained mimicry of a mariner's travel account, the extract from Pierre, the carpenter, is satirized by the author in a way that highlights the unreflective colonial narrative. Relating the specifics of the slave trade they are engaged in before the Commandant puts a hypocritical halt to it, Pierre expresses disdain for the manner in which some slaves react to their entry into the market. One woman, in particular, upon being separated from her family,

> *was wild and showing such a fury of strength as did surpass that of any man, biting and spitting and screaming her refusal in the Captain's face; and like it was a final impertinence to those who would separate her from her man and sons, she thereupon began to empty her bowels, excreting filth and passing out a mighty stream of her urine for all to see and in a manner which held no hint of discretion for those who witness such bestial forms of showing grief.* (118, emphasis in original)

The Swiftian moment in which the scatalogical body expresses better than her screams the woman's reaction to slavery—a response that was usually multiplied in the noxious slave holds—wounds Pierre's sensibilities. One of the most exquisite ironies of British colonialism, in particular, was the indefatigable expectation of civility in moments such as these. Lamming exploits the comic pretensions of genteel expectations from a carpenter who is quite offended by the ungrateful natives who neither appreciate the supposedly benign nature of the colonial transaction nor seem able to master the proper ways of expressing their displeasure with it. Pierre is thus able to elevate himself over the more brutish slaves by posing as the gentleman slaver.

In *Natives* the myths of imperialism weave through the actual history to thicken and tangle the linear thread of colonialist myth-as-history. Allegory is literally "other speaking." Writing from the point of view of the colonizers, Lamming nevertheless allows his sympathies for the colonized to come through, and the multiple systems of significations made possible by such a strategy reveal that both history and fiction are open to challenge. Apparently giving voice once more to the colonial voyagers, the iterative nature of the text ultimately undermines the point of view it assumes.

As Priest confesses in the final voyage, *"a whole world broke into fragments, and before my very eyes"* (322, emphasis in original). The readers of the novel are forced to confront lapses in historical memory, and, conversely, Priest is forced to forget the meaning of his history. While the natives are shown to be silenced by the act of colonization, in a reciprocal act, the catastrophic events that disestablish the colony render Priest wordless and his past futile:

> And all my past, the whole history of my service, has finally deprived me of all meaning. I watch the words I can no longer name, and realize I am simply exercising with the alphabet. . . . My body is already like a corpse, nameless and without any memory of its former substance. (323, emphasis in original)

The wounded, emptied subject that has *"lost all power to pray"* replaces the whole and hallowed self that sought to civilize the savages. Priest's agonized psychological disintegration carries along with it the ruined corpus of the authoritative text and the grand enterprise. This journey will not culminate in a return that will legitimate the passage. The categorical reliability of the eyewitness is dismantled through his inability to testify with any certainty of self or history. I do not mean to underestimate the recorded triumphs of the passage of colonial capital and to suggest that with this one novel Lamming successfully heals the wounds of its history. Rather, his refusal to categorize uninterrupted victory is a potent reminder that there was more to the grand narratives than they themselves allowed. If divinely inspired utterance sanctioned the discourse of empire, the loss of speech in one of its major representatives deliberately mutilates the rhetoric of sovereignty.

Priest's confession of powerlessness and silence signals the final humiliation of a glorious journey. In yet another irony, the secrecy and stealth of the entire operation make it nonexistent in the official documents of the Kingdom of Lime Stone. The sole witness onboard, Pinteados, refuses to sign any record of the final events. The enterprise therefore loses its citation, its documentary flourish, the conclusive announcement of the name and identity of the survivor that establishes verity in several accounts in Hakluyt's *Voyages* and seals the successfully undertaken voyage. Significantly, this narrative of failure remains unknown to the colonial power. In the novel, the text and instruments of empire are refused authority and significance and are dismissed and erased by the lack of print, as Anderson might note, on the single sheet of paper:

> A brilliance of morning raged over the charts and pierced the globe that rose like a human head from the council table. Broken shadows of blood burnt black along the edge of the table. The trail continued over the floor, swerving past the small bed, until it reached the door. A blank sheet of paper lay curled in the far corner. Dry stains covered its surface like cakes of mud. It was less than an hour since they had disposed of the bodies. (310–11)

The explicit performative of the signature disappears with as little ceremony as the performers, leaving only the signs of violence as cryptic evidence of the officers' existence. The withdrawal of the proper name undermines institutional authority, and the secrecy in which the journey is made remains its final shroud for the colonial authorities of Lime Stone.

Chapter 2

Inside the Trojan Horse: England Beseiged in *The Emigrants* and *Water With Berries*

Yes, it is wonderful to be British—until one comes to Britain.
—E. R. Brathwaite, *To Sir, With Love*

In his brief preface to *Beyond a Boundary*, C. L. R. James identifies England as the terminal point in his geographical and intellectual travels: "If the ideas originated in the West Indies it was only in England and in English life and history that I was able to track them down and test them. To establish his own identity, Caliban, after three centuries, must himself pioneer into regions Caesar never knew."[1] Lamming's focus on the sea voyage in *Natives* marks the initial stages of the later journey that James alludes to, setting the scene for the immigration of West Indians hundreds of years after the slaving and settlement enterprises on the islands. Migration outward is not a modern phenomenon in the Caribbean, but the forces underlying James's reverse voyage for "Caliban" are unique to the colonial subject whose initial loss of space, identity, value, and history apparently demands the pursuit of "Prospero" into the so-called mother country, once a space colonized by the distant Caesar. Both Lamming and James rationalize the inevitability of reversing colonial trajectories by pointing to the effects of colonial education on West Indian intellectuals, centered as it was on British history and culture. Once within the inviting imperial metropolis, the lost or unsettled identity of these intellectuals could rechart its blurred borders.

George Lamming's novels, *The Emigrants* and *Water With Berries*, published in 1954 and 1971, respectively, begin with James's premise,

55

but go on to make his migratory triumph more problematic. The novelist also includes other reasons for the phenomenon of West Indian migration in the fifties, implying that economic reasons were just as crucial as ideologically influenced notions of Britain's greatness. While the search for a valid historical space might impel immigrants to move beyond their national boundaries, the success of the search is not as inevitable as the teleology assumes. Although Lamming is not blind to "the pleasures of exile,"[2] the paradox of the privilege is that neither the confusion about history nor the alienation from a coherent sense of nation and identity disappears. Ironically, the self-discovery that James valorizes in the migration only brings to crisis the doubts and anxieties that drove one to the colonial metropolis in the first place. Both of Lamming's novels present a grimmer picture of Caliban's pursuit of the dream of England, a dream that, for at least Lamming's group of immigrants, turns out to be just one more nightmare of colonial history.

In an illuminating account of the anticolonial implications of the Prospero-Caliban trope, Rob Nixon concludes his article, "Caribbean and African Appropriations of *The Tempest*," by arguing that the play no longer has the same significance that it once had for postcolonial writers, not only because of its extensive rewriting, but also due to its inability to address contemporary realities. According to Nixon, the Calibanesque "spirit of insurrection" has been momentarily sated by Prospero's departure for his country (the withdrawal of colonial presence), Caliban's recovery of his island (independence in almost all colonized countries), and the demystification of Prospero's (the empire's) cultural and economic superiority. As Nixon explains,

> For in that turbulent and intensively reactive phase of Caribbean and African history [between the late fifties and early seventies of this century], *The Tempest* came to serve as a Trojan horse, whereby cultures barred from the citadel of "universal" Western values could win entry and assail those global pretensions from within.[3]

While agreeing with Nixon's account of cultural subversion in discursive contexts, I believe that the "sixth act" to the drama of the Trojan horse is enacted in the literal migration to the metropolis, through which not just the text but the immigrants themselves operate from the belly of the beast. The transgression of boundaries celebrated by James is met with deep foreboding in England, as the nation fears that its sanctified citadels are being undermined by the colonial exodus. In other words, while the empire writing back with a vengeance was bad enough, when it literally comes home to roost within its national borders, Nixon's analogy of the Trojan horse gains far more threatening dimensions. As "a colonial and exiled descendant of Caliban in the twentieth century," Lamming suggests that the war is far from over—the reverse passage to England has its own drama to narrate.[4]

James and Lamming were not alone in their conviction that, for various reasons, West Indians of a particular generation had no alternative but *"to get out."*[5] While V. S. Naipaul's Sisyphean account of the West Indies in *The Middle Passage* is characteristically bleak, claiming that narrative there is silenced and history submerged, Lamming, who initially claims a similar sense of hopelessness and frustration, refuses to conclude with England's triumph. Whereas Naipaul's discourse converges with Powellian characterizations of a mindless and vampirish dependence of the Third World on the metropolis, Lamming more self-consciously critiques the inherited structures of neocolonial dependency complexes and refuses to place the First World in a hallowed position. Instead, he historicizes the impoverishment of the colonies, and he underlines the benefits of labor, art, and other cultural resources taken from the so-called dependent countries.

"In Jamaica," says Naipaul, "my diary entries grew shorter and shorter and then stopped altogether. There was nothing new to record. Every day I saw the same things—unemployment, ugliness, over-population, race—and everyday I heard the same circular arguments."[6] Initially, *The Emigrants* seems to echo this sense of ahistoricity on the islands, repeating with few variations the statement, "we were all waiting for something to happen."[7] But the novel's conclusion in England is unable to move beyond a similar deferral, suspending both narrative and history in the uncertain expectancy of the opening chapter. The liminal tensions one perceives in the "small islands" are therefore not dissolved at the end of the rainbow, but rather reconfigured into a new ambivalence that also rejects celebration. Similarly, the explosion of crises in *Water With Berries*, a phrase borrowed directly from Caliban's poetic speech of accusation, stops short of a final conclusion, only predicting racial tensions in the metropolis and a possible revolution on Lamming's imaginary, composite West Indian island, San Cristobal. The initial promise of migration eventually unveils itself as the curse of the Middle Passage, as *Natives* proves, on both sides of the colonizer-colonized divide. Lamming's choice of a title from Caliban's oft-cited retort to Prospero's claims of nurturing Caliban and of the latter's subsequent ingratitude indirectly extends the scornful rejection of colonial nurture to England's colonial role. The title focuses, instead, on Caliban's sense of grievance, on his welcoming Prospero to his island and revealing to him its "qualities," and on the system of exchange with Prospero, who educates Caliban, only to deceive him through his culture, to make him drunk on it. As Caliban argues in *The Tempest:*

> This island's mine by Sycorax my mother
> Which thou tak'st from me. When thou cam'st first,
> Thou strok'st me, and made much of me, wouldst give me
> Water with berries in't, and teach me how
> To name the bigger light, and how the less,
> That burn by day and night, and then I lov'd thee
> And show'd thee all the qualities o' th' isle,
> The fresh springs, brine-pits, barren place and fertile:
> Curs'd be I that did so![8]

London proves to be as treacherous a space for the new Calibans in Lamming's novels. While the economic deprivation on the islands have made the literary enterprise there a marginal one, the exiled status of West Indian artists in London and their racial difference result in other tensions that work against their productivity and fair intellectual or labor exchange. Unlike James, therefore, Lamming suggests that questions raised in one space do not necessarily find their answers in another. Rather, England itself poses a whole new series of questions to the migrants who believe that within its portals lies history.

To borrow Fanon's distinction between the settler space and the native space, just as the native in the impoverished shanty space casts envious eyes at the settler's town,[9] the potential migrant views the industrial metropolis with desire. Using a diagnosis similar to Fanon's, Ambalavaner Sivanandan argues that in general the metropolis "was a well-fed world, free, healthy, full of good things, of laughter, of children growing straight and strong, while [the colonial periphery] was stricken with hunger and disease, and [its] children wizened at birth."[10] Such perceptions form the background to a voluminous literature of exile and migration, extending material deprivation to loss of history. The epigraph to one such novel by Caryl Phillips, *The Final Passage,*[11] quotes T. S. Eliot, portraying, more ironically than James, the questions of historic belonging that fuel colonial immigration:

> A people without history
> Is not redeemed from time, for history is a pattern
> Of timeless moments. So, while the light fails
> On a winter's afternoon, in a secluded chapel
> History is now and England.[12]

In the colonies, emulating the values of the empire could not but make England a particularly alluring lodestar guiding the course to "history." The long lines at harbors, consulates, and airports; the pictures of anxious travelers deposited at Southampton and later Heathrow; and the significance of "departure" and "arrival" in the modern appendix (or the sixth act) to the narrative of colonialism are all familiar scenes in many Caribbean texts.

Migration has long been a survival strategy in the economically dependent Caribbean islands. Lamming suggests as much in the conclusion to his first novel, *In the Castle of My Skin,* which, mirroring his own life, ends the high school career of his protagonist, G., with his departure to Trinidad. In an apparent continuation of the trajectory, *The Emigrants,* his second novel, has a first-person narrator leaving one of the islands on a ship that is on its way to England. A later ship to England is called the *Golden Image,* the name an ironic reflection of London and a parody of the economic hopes resting in the mammon of the colonial metropolis, long worshipped and desired by the immigrants. The mythification of the "mother country" is undermined by the pessimistic tone of the narrator, who soon merges into a third-person narrative. The gradual disappearance of the "I" repeats a characteristic narrative strategy of Lamming's, combining the individual and the collective to indicate a representative situation: all of them in the same boat, figuratively and literally speaking. Nevertheless, such a merging of voices rarely indicates unity and coherence of character and voice in any of Lamming's novels. Rather, passages detailing the gradual disintegration and objectification of the individual subject are repeated in various novels, splitting the "I" until it dissolves into a third-person singular or plural.

In *The Emigrants,* the first-person voice introduces the idea of objectification, a recurrent trope in the novel, and almost immediately

fades, allowing the third-person account to take over. Obsessing about
the elusive Queenie, one of the passengers onboard, the first-person
narrator says, "I didn't see her on the deck that evening, and I never
saw her till the ship reached England almost a fortnight later, but
throughout the voyage the presence of the object, her body, was on the
deck, and I kept it, naked under the sun, before my eye." The foreshadowing of Collis's later psychosis and Higgins's persecution mania
through the betrayal of hopes, and through a misguided trust in the
guiding spirit of the metropolis, follows from the continuing but
blurred sense of watching and being watched: "Darkness and the
steeple and the walls of the deserted church: these became one with the
water and the ship and again the girl in her nakedness under the sun,
all bundled in a blur beneath the cross and the words: / Father Into Thy
Hands I Commend My *Spirit*" (24, emphasis in original). The sexist surveillance of Queenie's body is followed by the "object-ive" third-person narrative. The first-person voice predicts the unraveling of Collis's
sanity, and it is perhaps not irrelevant that Collis, most identified with
the "I," loses sense not only of self, but also of vision.

The ship itself comes to configure a compressed Caribbean assort-
ment, through which, in a faint echo of the more traumatic Middle Passage, a number of different groups are forced into close communion. Of
course, while specific differences between them create schisms, the
immigrants themselves will be read as a coagulated, faceless mass in
the metropolis. Distinctions based on the different sizes of the islands
from which they come disappear because, as far as the "big island" is
concerned, "education or no education, the whole blasted lot o' you is
small islanders," as the Governor impatiently tells the squabbling
island nationalists (38). Eventually, the nation as a category is super-
seded by the federation, and the specific island identity for a "West
Indian" one. Asserting that the need to articulate a common identity
emerges from a crisis in history, the Jamaican's remarks in the dramatic
dialogue onboard depict the upheaval through the metaphor of
national vomit. What is distinct about this violent discharge is that it
owes its existence to what has been thrown up by a number of
nations—England, France, Spain, China, India, and, of course, a great
number of African countries. "Them is West Indians. Them all provin'
something. An' is the reason West Indies may out o' dat vomit produce
a great people, 'cause them provin' that them want to be something"
(66). The Jamaican asserts the possibility of productive history in spite

of its beginnings in terror and exploitation. Nevertheless, the journey itself is rooted in flight from that heritage and in anticipation of a more celebratory space elsewhere. Immigrants pursuing the quest to make something of themselves find that they are equally, if not more, indigestible in the interior of London.

While Ernest Renan's concept of the nation relies on a rich heritage, a grand past, and noteworthy national heroes,[13] the migration to England is, as I have said, impelled by the perceived lack of such "social capital" on the islands. In *Water With Berries*, Roger is unable to regard San Cristobal as "human soil," since it seemed to have "no antiquity; no magic of remoteness; no trail which led to some prize of ruins that might be waiting for discovery."[14] Traced in the architectural tropes of Lamming's novels, the conditions of possibility are themselves constrained both by the lack of ancient monuments and by the ruins of modern development. The nation cannot trace its history backward to antiquity nor can it seem to move any further into the future. For the immigrants, what the Strange Man shouts in his hasty scramble to get onboard may say it all: "what you want to leave me in dis Godforsaken place for?" (*The Emigrants*, 13). The continued references early in the novel to "a better break" reinforces the urge to escape, to find a more productive life in the mother country, and to break away from the perceived sterility of the islands. "It mattered to be in England. Yes. It did matter" (107). However, the eventual breakdown of Collis's vision, where he is unable to distinguish the person from the object, challenges the immigrants' belief that here their problems will be resolved, they will find a sense of historical agency, and they will, in spite of news of housing problems, find a more receptive home.

The title, Little England, affixed to Barbados, Lamming's native island, aptly sums up the colonial relationship between the supposed offspring and the mother country, (Big) England. As the schoolboys demonstrate in *In the Castle*, celebrating Empire Day with gusto, saluting the British flag, reading more British history than local history, and being told that a scholarship to a British university or a job in England is the apex of scholastic and economic achievement—all these experiences not surprisingly influence these children to believe that history and the significance of their own lives must stop beyond a certain point on the islands. As the narrator says in *Water With Berries*, "from the beginning they had been educated for escape" (69). The colonial masters, having treated them like children, had created an environment of

arrested adolescence, a fear that nothing productive lay outside of England, a conviction echoed by James that all roads lead there. Moreover,
as *In the Castle* and *Of Age and Innocence* accurately represent, when
riots and uprisings merely lead to a neocolonial power structure, economic and political equities seem unlikely in the colonies. Having been
taught all through school that England was the greatest nation, that it
dominated world history, and that it alone had any worthy culture, the
next logical move seemed to be the one that James suggests—to go to
England and "test" these ideas. In Merle Hodge's *Crick Crack, Monkey*,
the sea change in a snobbish school when Tee prepares to leave for England is still a familiar reaction in former colonies. Initially dismissed for
not belonging to the elite, coded circles of class, color, and urban privilege, Tee is fawned over by the same people who had ignored her earlier, once they learn that she is leaving for England. Like Lamming's
immigrants, Tee believes she has no choice but to leave: "Everything
was changing, unrecognizable, pushing me out. This was as it should
be, since I had moved up and no longer had any place here. But it was
painful, and I longed all the more to be on my way." The last line of the
novel expresses a desire for flight, captured in the image of the plane
taking off for England.[15] Gaining entry into the haughty domain of the
imperial metropolis becomes an achievement in itself.[16]

In ironic ways, part of England's "great past" literally comes back
to haunt it on home territory. As Kobena Mercer succinctly puts it, *"we
are here because you were there."*[17] This carnivalesque reversal is celebrated in Louise Bennett's "Colonization in Reverse," a poem that
repeats the image of the empire striking back:

> Dem a pour out a Jamaica;
> Everybody future plan
> Is fi get a big-time job
> An settle in de motherlan.
>
> What an islan! What a people!
> Man an woman, ole an young
> Jussa pack dem bag and baggage
> An tun history upside dung![18]

But the immigrants are far from conquering hordes that sweep all
before them, although the metropolis itself would like to believe so.[19] In

The Emigrants, the momentary triumph of entry rapidly disappears, as embodied by the disconnected narrative. The prose breaks up into poetic repetition, echoing the modernist alienation of Eliot's *The Waste Land,* and the train journey leading the immigrants to their destinations compresses the insights they will painfully learn about their dream space. In describing the journey, Lamming refers to the war, not just because it was after World War II that the first significant influx of colored immigrants began, but also because living in England is itself adapting to a state of war:

> Now
> you are in the war zone. England. Am I really
> in England. Remember the battles. England
> was always the place that fought battles, the
> country with some enemy . . .
> It was Britons, Britons never shall be
> slaves. This is England. . . . (119–20)

In the later novel, *Water With Berries,* the vast and complex urban topography of London provides a base for planning war against neo-colonial rule. The members of the Secret Gathering who meet periodically to plan a series of revolts back on the islands are presented as guerrillas plotting military strategies in the subterranean space of the city. As Lamming insists both in his novels and in his interviews, the sojourn in England turns out to be an essential test, not in the Jamesian sense of validating ideas, but in forcing the immigrants to respond to the myth of England as a safe haven. In the three novels in which Lamming specifically deals with immigrants in or returning from the metropolis, the explosion of the "idea of England" initiates a sense of identity that now negotiates not just the inadequacies of the island economies, but also the racial hostility of their mythicized space. In *Water,* for instance, Derek is metaphorically shot with the "bullet" of racial abuse that suddenly emerges from O'Donnell, a drinking buddy at the pub. As in *Natives,* O'Donnell's abuse exposes the interlocking systems of racism and sexism, as words like "coon," "nigger," "coolie shit," "bitch," "whore," and "white trash" allow him to vent his rage against black men and white women (*Water With Berries,* 209). The second part of the novel is appropriately titled "Under the Veil," a phrase that signifies on the title of Lamming's first novel, *In the Castle of My*

Skin. He continues to use the skin as a socially constructed site open to attack and to expose what lies hidden under the veneer of civil society.

The economic realities of unemployment and housing shortages are compounded by the discrimination the immigrants face in *The Emigrants.* "Why do so many of your people come here?" is a question that exemplifies the popular attitude to colored migrant and settler labor in England (141). Asked by Mr. Pearson with apparently genuine confusion, it assumes that the invasiveness of colonialism was one thing and the migration of the colonized is another. Such a question is perhaps what Mercer anticipates when he categorically states, "we are here because you were there." But this is not an answer calculated to appease the sense of threat excited by the visible presence of colored bodies. Although migration before independence in the colonies was officially allowed since the migrants were members of the Commonwealth, as immigration increased, the grand rhetoric of the empire-nation disappeared as its very skin began to take on a dramatic change. The paternalistic, federalist narrative of imperial destiny was replaced by the discourse of lamentation (a merry old England is losing its strong national character), of fear (the aliens are taking over), and of anger ("they" are responsible for all "our" problems, racial and otherwise). The homogenization of whiteness and Britishness was accompanied by a homogenization of blackness and non-Britishness, excluding nonwhites from national belonging. In the British context, the distinction between Asian and Afro-Caribbean immigrants disappeared from time to time as they were all seen as absolutely, racially other, similar only in their difference to English whiteness. If a sense of national pride was unavailable in the small islands, as the immigrants were soon to find, it was not very forthcoming in the big one either.

Immigration to Britain has a long and turbulent history, contrary to the general perception that it is a modern phenomenon. Racialized and nationalistic reactions to immigration were by no means a first with the Caribbean populations in the fifties, although they gained their current, crystallized forms with them. Anti-Irish and anti-Semitic rhetoric accompanied measures against earlier waves of migration. The Aliens Order of 1905 was a predecessor to later immigration controls, including the infamous 1962 Commonwealth Immigrants Act. But what was unique to the later measures was an increasingly widespread mobilization of a national idea and immigration policies based on color and race. In a nation that had little direct interaction with large numbers of dark-skinned people, the perception of being engulfed by what seemed to be a sea of alien bodies was terrifying. Although England required the labor of the immigrants, they were unwanted guests to many of the "locals," who typically put up signs such as "Keep Britain White" and "No Colored" to get their message across until the 1968 Race Relations Act outlawed discriminatory signs.

The sexual connotations of such penetrations into hitherto safe terrain were stereotypically represented in metaphors of rape, infection, and impurity. The construction of the a priori criminal was especially pertinent to the militant West Indians, who were perceived as threatening even by other people of color. Ironically, all people of color were read unvaryingly as black, a term later appropriated by activist intellectuals of color to assert solidarity, only to be abandoned later. However, splits within the groups along national, continental, and gender lines are apparent in *The Emigrants*, when the black West Indian women, for instance, react with hostility to the demands of their male counterparts, as well as to the African, Azi. In a peculiar reversal also embodying the splits in black consciousness, Azi is simply "the African," with a name but no nationality, whereas some West Indian characters such as "the Jamaican" are individually identified by their nation rather than by their personal name.

Although Lamming's reference to Caliban as his literary predecessor makes the latter singular and homogeneous, the characters in the novel, while claiming a common identity, are critical of the leveling of their distinct communities into a universal and usually disreputable similarity. In the dialogue between the policeman and the customers at the barber's shop, much confusion is caused by the label "your people." The Jamaican himself is not surprised by the assumption that there would be a "natural" connection between Higgins, suspected of drug dealing, and the rest of the group. Since they have all been categorized by the color of their skin, the belief that "there is some black underground connecting every one of us" is inevitable, he concludes bitterly (*The Emigrants*, 163).

Lamming both challenges and perpetuates the sexual and racial stereotypes, intimately intertwining black and white, male and female, and African, Afro-Caribbean, and Indo-Caribbean characters in complicated relationships in *The Emigrants* and in *Water With Berries*. The "drug" that Higgins is carrying, as it turns out in the former novel, is only a bizarre potion that Azi has concocted to cure Frederick, who is white British, of his impotence. The ménage à trois with Frederick's white partner, Peggy, is also meant to help, although the explicitly sexual and interracial encounter eventually reduces Frederick to a voyeur. Interestingly, Phillip jumps to the conclusion that Frederick is insane, a suspicion that several characters in the novel share about each other. The concatenation of madness, sexuality, and violence leads to explosive crises in both novels, each dramatizing Lamming's sense of the prevalent disease of colonialism and, at the same time, ironically representing the discourse of colonialism, which has traditionally associated madness, illness, and promiscuity with the colonies. Derangement and estrangement become interchangeable conditions in those characters who literally break down in the course of their struggle to survive in the hostile metropolis. Once urged to be patriotic to the British empire, the outsiders-turned-insiders now necessitate the practice of colonization *within* the borders of England. As John Solomos and others claim in their opening discussion in *The Empire Strikes Back,* what was distinct about postwar racism and internal colonization was that they were tinged with the paranoia of a weakened empire and a declining nation-state that could not cope with the insidious presence of the "enemy within."[20] In the same collection, Errol Lawrence, mimicking the classical horror of conquest, puts it thus: "The 'barbarians' are no longer 'at the gates,' they are within the city itself!"[21]

Water With Berries more specifically allegorizes the decline of empire, according to Lamming in two different interviews with George Kent and Daryl Cumber Dance.[22] Problematically, he chooses to personify colonial "impotence" in the figure of the Old Dowager, Mrs. Gore-Brittain, whose tenant, Teeton, seeks to return to San Cristobal to participate in the emergent national revolution. The aging matriarch is meant to be a symbolic comment on England's waning power, reproducing the woman as absence, as castrated masculinity. The feminized erosion of strength also uncovers the dangers and limitations of the Caliban trope in postcolonial rewriting, foregrounding as it does the angry colonized male as protagonist and an enfeebled old woman as the weakening empire.

While Lamming chastises Miranda, the other character interpellated by Prospero in *The Tempest,* for her inability to seek any commonality with Caliban, what happens to white women in *Water With Berries* tends to substantiate the divide. Lamming at first productively splits the Miranda figure in his novel in two: a white woman, Myra, and a black woman, Randa, each complicating the gender-race spectrum. But Myra is gang-raped in the novel by the servant-overseer, who mobilizes the sexually and economically abused servants of her supposed father, Fernando, in violent insurrection. Yet another rape-as-colonial-revenge is enacted by Derek onstage, when he sexually assaults an actress in full view of a shocked audience. In his interview with George Kent, Lamming talks of the rape as an exorcism of colonial usurpation. The ritual of forcefully entering the woman's body apparently cleanses the damaged psyche of characters such as Derek,[23] a black stage actor who is forced to play a corpse because he is judged inadequate for more substantial roles—an implied reflection of the reified colonizer-colonized roles in history. Lived performance of sexual assault is used to mitigate against performative stereotyping, but the black man as rapist is hardly a radical breakthrough against such stereotyping.

During his interview with Lamming, George Kent refers to Frantz Fanon, a reference made appropriate by Fanon's discussion of the white woman's objectified, emblematic status in the masculinized and racialized struggle between colonizer and colonized. "When my restless hands caress those white breasts, they grasp white civilization and dignity and make them mine," Fanon explains, representing the position of the colonized male.[24] Desire for the white woman, transferred from the desire for colonial power, is correspondingly reversed into violence against her and substituted for an attack against the white man whose property she becomes. In an all-too-familiar systemic flow of sexual aggression and assault, women embody a functional interruption of the man-against-man chain of violence. The frustrated colonized male seeks colonial redemption and a return to masculinity by turning against the nearest available woman. Reading the rapes as a necessary, if misguided, exorcism seems to echo the belief that the white woman is a therapeutic source of violence. "The rage inflicted on her [Myra] is really that intended for Prospero, for she cannot in the minds of Prospero's victims be separated from his privilege and his history," Lamming explains to Kent.[25] How then, one may ask, does Lamming expect Miranda to empathize with Caliban, who, rather than rejecting the accusation of rape leveled against him, is made to accept it with a leer?

Teeton's killing and burning of the Dowager are apparently one more method of expelling tyranny, except that in this case the Dowager, unlike the more troubled Myra, is a malignant force intent on controlling Teeton. While burning established sites of exploitation, such as canefields and the master's house, is a familiar act of resistance in the West Indies, *Water With Berries,* unlike *The Emigrants,* which portrays more canny women, tends to emphasize finally women as objects of terrible violence, justly or unjustly meted out to them. The accidental murder of Mrs. Belvedere in a sadomasochistic caning ritual that she pays for, the suicides of Nicole and Randa, the multiple rapes that Myra endures—all these events position women, black and white alike, as hapless victims of colonial conflict. Although women have certainly not been exempt from establishing and exploiting imperial structures, Lamming shows a testosterone-impelled resistance at work that ultimately restricts the power the women exercise. Not only is the empire figuratively depicted as female in its current weakened status, but having assumed that as a natural gendering, a violent rejection of colonization by the characters is then atomized into numerous attacks against women.

Male characters are not always the only ones responsible for using women as scapegoats. In *The Emigrants,* although Una Solomon, alias Miss Ursula Bis, is destroyed by Frederick's duplicity, she reacts by killing Queenie, who is also her lover but is perceived by Frederick as being morally responsible, along with Peggy, for Miss Bis's ravaging promiscuity. The lesbian interlude turns out to be a passing phase in Miss Bis's life, since Frederick decides to "rescue" her from further decadence by marrying her, not realizing that this physically transformed woman is the same one he virtually abandoned at the altar years ago on her native island. Miss Bis's pathetic story, targeted for satire by unsympathetic calypsonians, highlights the consequences of color and class obsession on the islands, compelling her to turn to a white man whose name might give her the status she desires. A characteristic strategy of Lamming's novels is the deferred disclosure, usually of a secret, as in Una/Miss Bis's case, revealed in a series of disconnected events and confessions. The unexpected behavior of characters constantly catches the reader off guard, unsettling complacencies just when it seems one knows what's coming. Thus while the entire episode emphasizes, as it does in Derek's case, that decolonizing violence is often self-destructive and internecine, the continual shock of revelation-in-installments makes both plotting colonial relationships and following the plot of the novel a difficult experience. While revenge and murder are themselves familiar plot devices in postcolonial literatures, the erotic, tense intimacies of hetero and lesbian relationships disrupt the homogeneity imposed on the immigrants, transgressing the neat categories of nation, sexuality, and identity. Nevertheless, the characters play into perceived notions even as they attempt to disrupt stereotypes. Killing the supposed perpetrator of lesbian "infection" to prove agency is eventually as torpid a strategy as Derek's attempt at revolutionary violence.

In allegorically representing and transforming the story of Caliban from its dramatic form to his prose version, Lamming forces the trope out of its restricted context into a statement on the consequences of colonialism. In the play, Caliban's curse is the consequence of being cheated, a curse he calls down upon himself. It is also his rhetorical strategy, turning to language as an acquired weapon used against his tyrannical tutor to shriek abuse and condemnation. In *The Pleasures of Exile,* Lamming's discussion of *The Tempest* in its colonial implications reveals its stance in the title of his chapter, "A Monster, A Child, A Slave," in which it is clear that the the monster is none other than Prospero, since Caliban is obviously the slave. In *Water With Berries,* Lamming continues to overturn the traditional interpretations of the civilized man of reason/enlightenment in Prospero and of the savage in Caliban. While Fernando, the brother of the Prospero figure in the novel, refers to the natives of San Cristobal as monsters, he includes his brother as part of this group. Myra herself is stolen from the Old Dowager by her husband and, in another startling revelation, turns out to be the illegitimate daughter of her supposed uncle Fernando and Mrs. Gore-Brittain.

Lamming's various speculations in *Pleasures* about Prospero's mysterious wife and about the sexual relationships between Miranda and Prospero and Miranda and Caliban on the isolated island are given free rein in the novel. Prospero's wife, according to Lamming, has as much potential as her husband to be a domineering aristocrat. In the Old Dowager, though, the emphasis is on the maternal solicitude and overprotection that endanger Teeton's independence. Significantly, it is not the Caliban figure who turns hostile when rejected, but the feminine version of Prospero that cannot bear to be cast off. The allegorical implications of a modern recasting are made clear in the very beginning of *Water With Berries.* The split tree trunk that looks like a mutilated man, the white plaster head of Columbus, the maps screening the window that looks out onto the city, Teeton's room that is as "cosy as a cave," all function as props reconfiguring the colonial relationship in its modern variation—after independence, inside the metropolis, overseen by the facade of care and concern exhibited by Mrs. Gore-Brittain. The Ariel figure in the text, a hapless, delicate Nicole, who tries to mediate between races, genders, and nationalities, is buried under the remains of the tree trunk in the garden, a portent of the failure of mediation and an implacable sign of the disasters that conclude the novel.

Lamming's play on canonical narratives also includes the use of *Othello* as a challenge to popular racial tropes. Derek's one role that "fits," predictably, is the role of the Noble Moor, though Teeton, who despises Othello, dismisses the tragic grandeur of the latter with a "noble my arse. . . ." Teeton is more inclined to read Othello as an "insecure . . . hired foreigner," desperate to please the hostile Venetians who regard him as an outsider (*Water With Berries*, 134). Othello's self-destructive insecurity is reproduced in Roger's relationship with his American wife, Nicole, whose white skin is ultimately rejected in Roger's fears of miscegenation. Whiteness is marked as diseased and destructive, demanding annihilation and reversing the usual racial divide in anxieties about miscegenation. When Teeton burns the remains of the Old Dowager, the text explicitly describes the burning of "pure whiteness" as her skin melts.

The return of Caliban and Othello as vengeful literary tropes, as a warning of fictional characters being rewritten by those they have figuratively represented, recalls the function of the subplot of Caliban's revolt in *The Tempest*. Prospero's recollection of the impending threat interrupts the hegemonic splendor of the Masque that he has constructed in order to impress a biddable Miranda and Ferdinand. The Masque disappears in the moment of aggravation, as Prospero is reminded of his slave's insurgency.

Discussing the reinscription of Caliban in later versions, Edward Said confirms Lamming's argument that the resurrection of the character retrieves the historicity of Caliban, pushing his typecast role into more challenging dimensions framed by postcolonial responses.[26] Similarly, in the reappropriation of the familiar voyage motif, both a historically and a metaphorically crucial one for the Caribbean, "the decolonizing native writer . . . re-experiences the quest-voyage motif from which he [sic] has been banished by means of the same trope carried over from the imperial into the new culture and adopted, reused, relived." Conrad's influence on a number of postcolonial writers gains a different inflection if read in the context of Said's discussion of "reinscription," illustrated by him in the works of Ngũgĩ wa Thiong'o and Tayeb Salih.[27] The quest in *Water With Berries*, although it does not include the literal voyage of *The Emigrants,* metaphorically remaps the trajectory of Conrad's *Heart of Darkness.* We are forcibly reminded of the gloomy London landscape against which Marlow describes his travels into the Congo, eventually deflecting "the horror" of the opening into the dark interior of the stereotypical African jungle. Lamming returns the misadventures of imperial rule to the seat of its power in London. Rather than repeat the narrative in Conrad's fictional representation of steamy mangroves and emaciated natives, Lamming describes the city in *Water With Berries* to demonstrate the territorial shift. Alluding to the flight of Roger and Derek, the unnamed narrator says:

> It must have been the longest journey they had ever made. . . .
> It was the slowest journey they had ever made.
> The city had become a huge and foreign mausoleum where they walked. A procession of avenues marched them past the houses that rose like vaults, where everyone was asleep and shut tight in. And miles away the wave of fire rode after them with its cargo of ruins from the past. The photographs of Stratford rose in a rubble of smoking frames; and the charred skeleton of the piano floated its chords up to the sky, lamenting the day they had ever made this crossing. It must have been the quietest journey they had ever made. (221)

The journey undertaken by the West Indian immigrants holds as much terror and fear as the one recorded by Marlow; the city is as constraining and inscrutable as the jungle; one crossing is as disastrous as the other. Roger's acts of arson spontaneously attack various symbols of city life in the modern urban jungle, no longer the civilized center of a shaky world, but rather the very heart of its disorder and darkness.

The conclusion to *The Emigrants* is similarly oppressive. It takes the reader back to the disoriented landscape in the opening lines, mapping both modern nodes of travel, not in James's happy sense of closure, but in a brooding sense of ruin. Not much difference is observed between the first landscape and the last landscape of the novel. In the opening lines, the third-person narrative—soon to be broken by a first-person voice—describes a fragmented scene embodying violent interruption: "A small building broke the neck of the pier where it made a sudden descent to the sea" (3). In the conclusion, having just witnessed the fiasco with the Governor's wife and his unexpected violence against

her, some characters are left "to tidy the mess." Others melt away into
the darkness in a general atmosphere of bewilderment and embarrassment. The Governor, in a return to the expectation of the beginning,
believes "something was bound to happen." Collis, ever the observer,
"returned to the window and watched the night slip by between the
night and the trees," says the narrator in the last line of the novel
(281–82).

Fernando's hysterical outburst to Teeton expresses the material
consequences of the history that first evoked Caliban's curse. Recognizing the magnitude of the colonial "experiment," Fernando moves
the discursive complaint of Caliban into the realm of a prophetic male-
diction: "A curse! And it will come back to plague my race until one of
us dies. That curse will always come back. Like how you've come here"
(*Water With Berries,* 229). While Fernando continues to place the blame
on the other, the narrative itself, following in the direction of *Natives,*
locates colonialism as a curse that will backfire against those who have
profited from it. The bleakness of *The Emigrants* and *Water With Berries*
draws the obverse picture to Bennett's carnivalesque celebration and
triumph of migration, a triumph negatively caricatured in anti-immi-
grant rhetoric of ravaging hordes sucking the lifeblood out of the long-
suffering metropolis. Trauma replaces triumph as the characters experience the perils of migration to a hostile city.

Many immigrants worked in unhealthy, crowded, and stressful
environments during the day, often attending exhausting night classes
in the hope of getting a better job. Initially barred from pubs and clubs,
greeted with suspicion and hostility, and deprived of familiar social
structures, many of them lived an alienated and intimidating existence.
For the educated intellectuals who may not have faced the same economic privations, the crisis of identity and the shock of the reality of
England often proved the breaking point.

The gradual schizophrenia of Collis, the mental breakdown suf-
fered by Dickson upon discovering he is little more than a sexual fetish,
and the persecution complex of Higgins in *The Emigrants* are all
instances of disintegrating identities pathologized by their experiences
in England. Higgins's speedy and unjust incarceration demonstrates
what Errol Francis calls "metropolitan anthropology" at work, through
which pseudoscientific and psychiatric discourses such as somatome-
try, psychometry, eugenics, and so on were utilized against black people by academic, state, and police agencies. Reversing the idea of where
the threat lies and for whom, the collection *Inside Babylon: The Caribbean*

Diaspora in Britain, which includes Francis's piece on "psychiatric racism,"[28] suggests that black people have more to fear in England than its white inhabitants, in spite of the prevailing notion of a nation beseiged by "outsiders" of color. Apart from everyday racism, they also have to cope with the harrassment from institutions designed to protect and serve the public. Contrary to their expectations of a sanctuary inside the mother country, Lamming's immigrants also reveal that fear is not just a white experience: "Weak. Frightened. They said it wouldn't / be so cold. So cold . . . so frightened / . . . so frightened . . . home . . . go . . . to / go back . . . home . . . only because / . . . this like . . . no . . . home . . ." (124). Indeed, as Tornado suggests, "we got to suffer first and then come together. If there is one thing England going teach all o' we is that there ain't no place like home no matter how bad home is" (76). The nostalgia for the home that one left behind is reinforced by the harsh realities of life in England, yet the return home is not as easily achieved as Tornado suggests, however useful the learning process of migration.

In both novels there are brief moments of productive resistance amidst the overpowering aridity, usually enacted in a subterranean space. The barber, the women at the hairdresser's, Tornado and his refusal to play happy black entertainer, the Secret Gathering, and Roger's arson all articulate a determined sense of oppositionality. The barber is most explicit in making the connection between personalized, everyday insults and the larger system of colonial power that makes such insults commonplace and commonsensical. "Dat's why we in all the colonies will fight. . . . 'Tis the time to fight," he declares, although the force of his vigor is immediately deflected by a skeptical Azi and by the events in *The Emigrants* (132). Suggestively, the cultural sites of struggle are largely underground ones, the most prominent trope being the basement, the locus of community and coherence.

In *Water With Berries,* unlike the paralysis in the earlier novel, there is an active although also underground movement to plan a revolution in San Cristobal. The secret meeting of the Gathering is rendered in dramatic dialogue, a narrative strategy Lamming frequently resorts to when the emphasis is on action, as in the dialogue between the schoolboys in *In the Castle.* Here England itself becomes an enabling Trojan horse, although unwittingly, forcing the migrants underground and thus providing secret sites for subversion. The conclusion of the meeting and the arrival of Fola of Forest Reserve provide an interesting interface to his novels, which are often interconnected. Could this be the same Fola of *Season of Adventure,* published a decade before *Water With Berries* and also dealing with an overthrow of the neocolonial elites? The recollection of another novel and an earlier stage of revolt suggests a continued struggle against a treacherous state and government. While Lamming constantly defers and defuses revolution, he apparently seeks, at the same time, to emphasize continual resistance.

Teeton's desire to return home and directly participate in the planned violent revolution, proceeding further from Tornado's more nostalgic hope of return, raises the issue of the responsibility of artists and the degree of their involvement in national politics. While Teeton, unlike Tornado, at first expresses no resentment against England, instead considering it "a city of welcome, the safest harbour for his kind of waiting" (11), there is little doubt that he, like his other artist friends, believes his talents are wasted in the metropolis because of its racism. Although Lamming, along with other Caribbean writers, particularly Naipaul, achieved literary and commercial success in London, his own return to the Caribbean was motivated by a disillusionment with England and by a subsequent political commitment to the Caribbean. He confessed twenty years after he published his first novel, "Today I shudder to think how a country, so foreign to our own instincts, could have achieved the miracle of being called Mother. It made us pupils to its language and its institutions, baptized us in the same religion. . . . Empire was not a very dirty word, and seemed to bear little relation to those forms of domination we now call imperialist."[29]

Yet Lamming does reserve for England a kind of paradoxical maternal status, reading the experience of exile in its belly, so to speak, as an emergent, if terrifying, condition of being and knowing. If James argues for the testing of ideas through a journey mythologized by England's status as historically significant terrain, Lamming tests the nature of such an assumption by reversing expectations of triumph. Instead, the journey becomes an educational experience—a lesson in history—countering the myths of colonial England. As Lamming explains,

> there have been men who grew up, not with a knowledge of Prospero's background and world, but with an idea of that world. And what is happening to them now is that they are experiencing in their consciousness the disintegration of that idea. The irrelevance and the falsity of that idea beside the hitherto obscured reality.[30]

Significantly, Lamming seems more interested in a "West Indian" identity than an island-nation one. Apparently believing that one can forge this identity outside of its geographical boundaries, he talks about exile as a painful gestating period. "In this sense, most West Indians of my generation were born in England. The category West Indian, formerly understood as a geographical term, now assumes cultural significance."[31] The awareness of a common history strikes the immigrants most strongly outside of their national boundaries, according to Lamming, and England itself plays a primary role in initiating a sense of difference from the British Commonwealth, a difference that is made coldly clear to them when they are in the mother country rather than outside of it.

Water With Berries therefore seems to posit the next logical step to James's teleology—the return of the intellectual—a stage that Lamming takes up more completely (although equally pessimistically as new complications arise after independence) in earlier novels, *Of Age and Innocence*, where Shephard and Mark return to impending independence, and *Season of Adventure*, where Chiki returns from the United States to a neocolonial society. In a conversation with Teeton, Jeremy expresses the conviction that while the earlier generation before independence had no alternative but to depart, the younger generation must return to the task of revolution and nation building. In a continuing teleological fashion, if what "mattered" in one stage of the colonial trajectory was England, Jeremy projects the next act: "what's important is that he came back" (*Water With Berries*, 91).

Teeton's inability to answer Jeremy's challenge directly, however, suggests that the myth of the celebrated return of the exile is no more promising than the myth of migration to England. The novel refuses to conclude categorically with Teeton's return to his native island, but merely shows him sailing away after he escapes from the Orkneys. The bodies pile up in the conclusion and, as in *The Emigrants*, the air is thick with tense anticipation even as everyone seems paralyzed. The expectation of legal trials places us once more in the nexus of uncertainties at the start of the journey.[32] On trial here, however, are not just the immigrants who have reacted violently to their historical situation, but the history that brought them to England in the first place. They have tracked their ideas down to England and "English life and history," but once there they find themselves trapped in the continuing nightmare of colonial history.

Part 2. Intellectuals

Chapter 3

Making History in
In the Castle of My Skin

> The settler makes history and is conscious of making it. And
> because he constantly refers to the history of his mother country,
> he clearly indicates that he himself is the extension of that mother
> country. Thus the history which he writes is not the history of the
> country which he plunders but the history of his own nation in
> regard to all that she skims off, all that she violates and starves.
> —Frantz Fanon, *The Wretched of the Earth*

George Lamming's first novel, *In the Castle of My Skin,* published in
1953, soon after his migration to England, examines the problems of
history and historiography in the colonial West Indies. Colonial history, as Fanon indicates in the above citation, was not just a transplanted but a badly translated version from the colonialist's point of
view.[1] In *Natives of My Person,* Lamming attacks both literary and historical misconceptions about the nature of colonialism, exposing the
latter as an enterprise with few, if any, redeeming factors. His other two
novels focusing on a later migration, *The Emigrants* and *Water With
Berries,* explore the consequences of assimilating colonial presupposi-
tions about historicity. Since historiography is concerned with the ways
in which we conceptualize our location in local and, today, global cultures as well as our place in the past and the present, these novels
explain the physical trajectory of migration to England as dictated by
the imperatives of the colonial writing of history. As Fanon implies, the
act of inscription involves an evacuation of more than the discursive
potential of the colonies: it includes the skimming off of material
resources along with the continuing displacement of West Indian peo-

79

ple. When reality is conceptualized through writing and shaped through economic policies with England as the ideological and material center, departure from the colonies is a predictable culmination of that reality. But if history and potential in the modern West Indies seemed irrevocably trapped in the colonial complex, Lamming sees a way out by presenting, in his novels, the resistance of oral and rural cultures that persist in the Caribbean.

Edward Baugh identifies *In the Castle* as the first piece of fiction in the West Indies that expresses the West Indian writers' quarrel with history. Baugh's classification locates Lamming's creative work at a critical juncture in the hostile relationship between European, or settler history, as Fanon decribes, and West Indian "historylessness," as Baugh names it. He uses history in several ways to modify his ironic sense of historylessness. First, the history with which, in his view, the West Indian writers quarrel is the authoritative document of the colonizers, the well-known record that legitimizes their conquest even as it displaces and disavows the colonized. The personal and communal identity and history of those outside the pale of the colonial center are therefore (un)marked in the dominant text of Eurocentric history by Baugh's corollary—"lessness." The muted voices and diminished presences of Amerindians, slaves, indentured servants, and other objects of imperial expansion allowed for the fixed representation of the West Indies as a place without a history except as narrativized from a colonialist point of view. In his allegorical parody, *Natives,* Lamming satirizes the exclusions of colonial history and, rather than give voice to what has been muted, chooses to undermine what has been unreflectively celebrated in the plunder of native history. Second, Baugh uses history to problematize the supposed historylessness of colonized populations, particularly when their own accounts are considered. His resistant sense of a West Indian literary quarrel with history[2] is articulated against the acute anxiety generated by what were once the more commonly circulated narratives—the contemptuous remarks of a Carlyle, Trollope, or Froude.[3] It directs attention to survival and struggle among the subordinate peoples as it ascribes to literary texts the task of reinterpreting constitutive moments of colonial history.

Lamming's use of the riots of the thirties in *In the Castle,* for instance, exemplifies the quarrel that Baugh identifies as characteristic of West Indian literary history and historiography. In antagonistic opposition to official colonial perceptions, the novel dramatizes the

1937 riots as significant chapters in the islands' political history, bringing to crisis the neglect of the lower classes, predominantly black in the novel. I read the riots both as concrete, material interruptions to the everyday business of colonial life and as disruptive narrative interventions into those blank spaces of history. The riots are also important biographical material, since Lamming's generation of writers grew up during these turbulent years and his memories of the riots and their aftermath stimulated, in part, the production of the novel. As Lamming himself claims, "The Novel has had a peculiar function in the Caribbean. The writer's preoccupation has been mainly with the poor; and fiction has served as a way of restoring these lives—this world of men and women from down below—to a proper order of attention."4 But such a restoration does not emerge smoothly, given the weight of colonial middle-class authority in both history and literature. The wresting of control from those who previously wielded the pen is thus accurately represented by Baugh's contestatory metaphor of quarreling with the preceding generations.

Although multiple histories and uses of history emerge in *In the Castle*, it is with Baugh's sense of history as "lessness" that the novel begins. The dissolution of the torrential rains and floods that greets G.'s eyes on his ninth birthday denies the possibility of celebrating either a past, a present, or a future: "as if in serious imitation of the waters that raced outside," G. observes in what we realize later are notes in his diary, "our lives . . . seemed to escape down an imaginary drain that was our future" (10). He has little knowledge of his past, his father, or most other members of his family. Instead, the novel begins, as it ends, with the unique and often forced mobility of Caribbean populations: many of his family members have migrated from the island in search of better employment. In his second novel, *The Emigrants,* Lamming explores in some depth the ironies of a history that makes such an absence of rootedness almost inevitable. But he provides an introductory context in his very first novel, which opens with an ominous, apocalyptic downpour.

In order to situate G. within the colonial context and see him, as Baugh does, as representative of his village community, we need to move a short distance away from the shack where G. and his mother live to the landlord's house perched on the hill. In contrast to G., whose birth, according to the narrator, "began with an almost total absence of family relations," the history of Mr. Creighton, after whose line the village is named, seems both immutable and progressive. The narrator, whose voice unobtrusively interchanges with G.'s first-person narrative, establishes the genealogy with a care that is not without mockery:

> An estate where fields of sugar cane had once crept like an open secret across the land had been converted into a village that absorbed some three thousand people. An English landowner, Mr. Creighton, had died, and the estate fell to his son through whom it passed to another son who in his turn died, surrendering it to yet another. Generations had lived and died in this remote corner of a small British colony, the oldest and least adulterated of British colonies: Barbados or Little England as it was called in the local school texts. To the east where the land rose gently to a hill, there was a large brick building surrounded by a wood and a high stone wall that bore bits of bottle along the top. The landlords lived there amidst the trees within the wall. (*Castle,* 25)

The organic and linear connectedness of Creighton's past, as well as that of England's, empowers him to be spatially and culturally located over and above the lesser mortals—the rent-paying tenants on his land. Baugh rightly points out the representative status of the characters: Creighton is to the villagers what Big England is to Little England. His elevated status originates from and is sustained by the sheer inflexibility of his personal history, the "naturalness" of the series of successions pushing and keeping the villagers down. In contrast to the rooted past and status of Creighton, G.'s familial history is shaky and diluted; yet the former emerges as dynamic and the latter seems static. G.'s memories of his past and his national history are "a blank," a sinking "cargo of episodes like a crew preferring scuttle to the consequences of survival" (11). The metonymic reference to the sea recalls the Middle Passage, an account of which is given later in the dream-vision of the Old Man, or Pa, and the point of entry for G.'s ancestors. The lack of historical agency attributed to slaves forms the foundation of G.'s own perception, just like Fola's in *Season of Adventure,* of slavery in the West Indies as "a blank." If the "watery waste" of the village flood dissolves the fragile foundations of village houses, by extension, the terror of the Middle Passage is accountable for the confused and shameful sense of an equally tenuous history.

In *The Pleasures of Exile,* Lamming discusses the place of monuments in reflecting, grounding, and shaping a cultural history. The non-West, particularly Africa, is once again identified by the absence of such monuments. Lamming quotes a passage from James Baldwin's *Notes of a Native Son* to illustrate the particular trauma of enduring a parent-child relationship when one is at best a "bastard of the West." Speaking of Shakespeare, Bach, Rembrandt, the Stones of Paris, the cathedral at Chartres, and so on, Baldwin mourns that these "were not really my creations; they did not contain my history; I might search in them in vain for ever for any reflection of myself; I was an interloper."[5] This sense of standing outside a hallowed and established center is echoed in Lamming's novel. Like Baldwin, the villagers in *In the Castle* look up in awe at the Great House, the domain of the landlord. To look in at all, they play the roles of stealthy "interlopers," creeping behind fences and stealing through woods to peep at the daily rituals in the house. Their position outside a constructed and legitimized space as envious and guilty spectators accurately represents their initial status vis-à-vis the dominant history and culture, the "castle" of the colonizers.

In a village where the majority of people form the landless proletariat, inhabiting dilapidated tenements precisely because of the color of their skin, vision from within "the castle of [one's] skin" must ironically be defined and controlled through that biological integument. Lamming's characteristically careful choice of titles is evident in this case as well. Just as the phrase "natives of my person" in Lamming's sixth novel challenges the self/other dichotomy of colonial vision and fractures the unified subject of the conventional travel narrative, the "castles" of both the landlord and the villagers in his first novel are revealed as permeable and vulnerable constructions. Lamming's use of irony as a narrative strategy in all his novels is particularly appropriate for the purpose of unwrapping layers of meaning that distance the signified from the signifier and historical narrative from truth. The ironic recognition of the constructed value of one's skin in the place one is made to occupy reveals just how the discursive and material stratifications of colonial practice both disguise and perpetuate the exploitative conditions that support it.

The question of constructing the kind of monuments, cathedrals and so on, that Baldwin's gaze is transfixed by seems incongruous given the purpose that repopulated and eventually transformed the topography of the islands: plantation labor. The slaves' own bodies

were as much beyond their control as the land and labor it would take
to build such monuments on the scale in which they were built in
Europe. Further, as Gordon K. Lewis reminds us, in spite of the fact that
the West Indies itself functions as a sinister background in novels like
Jane Eyre, many of the architectural and artistic creations of England—
the noble country mansions, for example—owed much to the wealth
generated from the islands.[6] The point was not that the slaves were
uncreative, but that they were not in control of what they produced.
Their productivity was manifested not in their lifestyles, but in the
lifestyles of others elsewhere.

In an article that reads the Judeo-Christian archetype of the Fall
into *In the Castle,* Carolyn T. Brown, using the stereotype of a rediscov-
ered Eden, describes life before the riots in the novel as "atemporal"
and "paradisiacal."[7] Yet there is nothing heavenly about the region that
the villagers perforce inhabit, the part of the countryside that the landlord's house overlooks. The white people live in Belleville, where
houses "were all bungalows high and wide with open galleries and
porticoes." The villagers live in shanties, with galvanized sheets of iron
for roofs, that are unpleasant in the heat and insubstantial in the mon-
soons, as Mr. Foster's "house" proves by sailing down the street during
the flood with him on the roof. The spatial positioning of the housing is
as telling as their structural appearance: the makeshift shacks lie pros-
trate *below* the lofty affluence of the landlord's dwelling, the locus of an
exalted deity who is beyond mortal reach. In view of Fanon's topologi-
cal distinction between the wealthy settler town and the poor native
town,[8] the gaze of the villagers into the privileged space of the landlord
is directed by a dream of taking the landlord's place, a dream that only
Slime and his companions come close to achieving.

The poverty of the village is maintained by the villagers' lack of
control over the means of production in both the village and the city.
Unable to own the land on which they are really squatters or have
shares in the shipping companies for which they work, the villagers
have no choice but to depend on the charity of the landlord, which is
insulting in its limited scope. Mr. Creighton, for example, offers Miss
Foster half a crown and a cup of tea when he hears about the watery
end of her house. The fact that he is lauded by Miss Foster for his generosity and concern suggests the unequal power relations between the
landlord and the villager. Significantly, she insults the landlord's overseer soon after this episode and targets him as the real problem. The

tensions with the hated overseer and the street brawls that erupt periodically disprove the myth of the village as a blissfully unruffled space.
At one point, when a conversation between two women leads to a fight,
the narrator believes that the "village . . . must have seemed like hell
itself" (106). At this point, the older generation at least are reduced to
internal squabbles while groveling before the landlord.

At the time *In the Castle* was being written in 1951, the black population, who formed the majority of the lower classes in Barbados, occupied the lowest stratum designed by the race and class hierarchy, with
white planters, traders, and merchants on the top and the white and
colored petty bourgeoisie below them. Since the planters had swiftly
taken over most of the arable land for sugar plantation during the initial period of colonization, the freed slaves and servants were left with
virtually nothing for independent settlement and cultivation, continuing instead to depend on their work as plantation labor. Within the ten-
antry system established by the planter oligarchy after Emancipation in
the 1830s, land ownership by black villagers in Barbados was almost
impossible. Hilary Beckles provides three reasons for their marginal
status even as late as the 1930s. First, the planters had bought up all
available land on the tiny but densely populated island. Second, in all
but a few cases they refused to sell to black people. And third, it was a
strategic move on the part of the metropolitan and local leadership to
keep the majority of the population tightly leashed and powerless by
making them landless, and through a franchise law on property rights,
unable to vote.[9]

In 1935, shortly before the period in which the novel is set,
although the peasants and laborers formed the majority of the population, the planters owned disproportionate amounts of land. Seventy-
five percent of the holdings of those other than the planters were less
than one acre, claims Eric Williams. To add to the difficulties of the
peasants, the land they did acquire was of poor quality, making subsis-
tence farming a process of arduous and often thankless labor. Williams
sums up the living conditions of the laborer in 1935 in the following
passage: "The weekly budget of the Barbadian labourer was less than
two dollars; of this food cost him seven cents a day. The Barbadian
labourer was fed worse than a goalbird; he could not afford milk in his
tea; said the planters, he did not like milk!"[10] Williams then goes on to
list the unsanitary and decrepit housing of the villagers, who had to
fight unhealthy labor and living conditions and inadequate diet in

order to survive. If it seemed to some a land of gentle showers and
beauteous gardens, as Nathaniel Weekes rhapsodizes in his poem,
"Barbados," clearly that view was limited to the minority landowners
and planters.[11] For the peasants, as the opening lines of *In the Castle*
demonstrate, life was often a struggle with hurricanes and disintegrating shacks. In fact, the first section of the novel is a sobering reminder
of a way of life that tourist brochures on the Caribbean take care to disguise. In the commonly advertised visions of the islands as a bountiful,
sunny paradise, one is invited to conclude that the Caribbean is the
place to be if uninterrupted enjoyment is one's goal. Meanwhile, emigration from the islands into other areas tells a different story about the
residents.

Though the villagers in Creighton's village live in poverty, there is
little in the beginning of the novel that suggests direct individual or collective rebellion. Rather, the Sunday School teacher's advice to her son
represents the other extreme: "There is nothing for us to do . . . but
rejoice in our bondage" (72). The initial lack of resistance in the novel
may be historicized as a consequence of both material and ideological
factors. Along with the economic powerlessness delineated by Beckles,
the intimate and paradoxically distanced structure of relationships
between the villagers and the landlord reveals the ideological bond
that maintains lack of power on the part of the rural population. In the
paternalistic identification that mediates the interaction between landlord and subordinates, many of the villagers, and significantly most of
the women in this novel, feel that the landlord has more claim to their
loyalty than their own people. Thus in a variation of Miss Foster's obse-
quious behavior to the landlord, G.'s mother and her friends bemoan
the children's lack of respect to a white man, exhibited by their laugh-
ing uproariously at his discomfiture when a fowl defecates all over
him. Ma later commiserates with the landlord for the disrespect shown
him both by the boys, who break into his property, and by the strikers,
who refuse to work for his company.

One among the many conversations between the boys recalls
Fanon's conception of history as written by the settler, the history of the
colonial authorities, of dominant British culture. Trumper bitterly tells
G. that on becoming aware of his race, "act as you should an' don't ask
Hist'ry why you is what you then see yourself to be, 'cause Hist'ry ain't
got no answers," and the history he refers to is the settler's history that
remains deaf and blind to their community (297). Trumper's emigra-

tion to the United States enables him to be more militantly conscious of the race issue, unlike the villagers. In *The Pleasures of Exile,* Lamming corroborates this peculiar lack of militant race politics and suggests that being a numerical majority had much to do with it, unlike in the United States or in England, where minority status in a white world exacerbated the economic and political exclusion of black people. Likening the racially tense situation in Notting Hill to the condition of war, Lamming, like Fanon, describes the muscular tension and tightening that follows the first indications of a racial encounter. In spite of his body's warning signals, however, Lamming believes that his West Indian upbringing necessarily dulls his instincts, unlike the African Americans, whose daily experiences as a minority in the United States actually allow them to "smell . . . the arriving odour" of racism.[12]

Although Eugene Genovese implies that the consensual relations of master-slave networks were, in the final analysis, determined more by class than by race,[13] *In the Castle* ultimately goes on to highlight the racial aspect in such willing reciprocity. The black villagers link themselves to their landlord because the racial connection among them ceases to operate in their respect for whiteness and because their own class position is naturalized into an irrevocable, even necesssary degradation. As the narrator observes, "the enemy was My People. My people are low-down nigger people. . . . The myth had eaten through their consciousness like moths through the pages of ageing documents" (26–27). In the culturally embroiled identities of race and class, being black means, for the most part, being lower class, and being both black and lower class reduces one to the ultimate dregs of social status. In the village, therefore, not only do the inhabitants painstakingly distinguish between shades of black, the term itself becomes an insult. At the end of a long discussion of fair skin, light skin, and clear skin, all in varying shades of black, G. categorizes his friend Boy Blue as the blackest of them all. He goes on to explain: "When you asked him why he was so black, he would answer with serious conviction: 'Just as I wus goin' to born the light went out.'" G. concludes, "The light, we admitted, had gone out for many of us" (128). G. implies that, ultimately, the finer shades of color distinction so carefully elaborated in the colonies merge into one indistinguishable shade in the colonial vision, as the migrants are to discover in *The Emigrants.*

In his introduction to *In the Castle,* Lamming discusses other ideological reasons for the novel's "tragic innocence." The novel's critical vision of England is dim, Lamming believes, because he, like many other West Indians of the period, accepted the myth of the gracious Mother Country that ruled righteously and ruled well.[14] The power of the distant metropolis was thus reinforced by the force of colonial mentality, which repeated on a national scale the paternalistic contract between the landlord and the villagers. As in *Natives,* Lamming pays some attention here to the role of religion in sanctioning the unspoken contract between Big England and Little England. God and the monarch are blessed in the same breath on Empire Day. The street ceremony of the born-again Christians, Ma's fatalistic acceptance of the futility of the struggle for land in the material world, the tragicomic anecdotes of Jon, Susie, Jen and Bambi, Bots, Bambina, and finally, the narrative of the garden and the empire circulated in school all testify to the intrusiveness of Christianity, often with disastrous results. But religion is not the only colonial prop detailed in the novel. The actual foundation for this prop Lamming identifies in the introduction as "that slave culture which has persisted through school and college, university and people's parliament."[15]

Lamming's juxtaposition of slave culture and education adds a significant dimension to the issues of a lack of history and revolutionary possibility. He reads slave culture negatively, not to dismiss the culture of the slaves, but to imply that the slave context, integral to the social formations of the islands, was to leave its mark on the process of education. Equally important is the fact that popular education was not available until the nineteenth century, and even then it was a privilege, not a right. But if one is to believe Hegel, the instituiton of slavery was itself an educational process and an orientation into history for the Africans. "What we properly understand by Africa, is the Unhistorical, Undeveloped Spirit, still involved in the condition of mere nature, and which had to be presented here only as on the threshold of the World's History," he declares in an oft-cited passage of *The Philosophy of History.* Shortly before this passage, Hegel asserts that the slavery to which millions of Africans were subjected was an educational experience that involved "becoming participant in a higher morality and the culture connected with it."[16]

The vague discussion of slavery in the novel (it becomes removed from history for the schoolchildren) and the Sunday School teacher's suggestion that they "rejoice" in their "bondage" encode and repeat the colonial narrative that eventually imposes a liminal history and culture on the colonized. Quite masterfully, their very acceptance of domination is configured in the Hegelian scheme as the necessary condition of development, in order to cross "the threshold of the World's History." Yet the crossing for millions of Africans into the promised circuit of history was an annihilating passage rather than a rite of knowledge: it involved violence and dismemberment, loss of identity, and cultural alienation.

Louis Althusser's theory of the ideological state apparatuses, including educational systems, as disciplinary sites that reproduce existing forces and conditions of production is particularly pertinent to the colonial situation.[17] In *In the Castle,* the fact that the village school is a compromised locus of (mis)education emerges in its structural resemblance to a slave ship and its military formation of school "squads." Just as the framework of the village speaks for the race-class edifice, the codified rituals of the school ceremonies attest to the domination of the colonial subjects. In fact, each school itself participates in the class divisions of the island: "The High School was intended to educate the children of the clerical and professional classes, while the village school served the needs of the villagers, who were poor, simple and without a very marked sense of social prestige," says the adolescent G. toward the end of the novel (218–19). His metaphor of education as a discontinuous "steeplechase in which the contestants had to take different hurdles" emphasizes the embedded competitiveness of a capitalist society, through which some children go on to reach the goalposts of middle-class bureaucracy and others aspire to the lesser status of vocational trades (218). As his later novels suggest, Lamming indicates another destination, illustrated by the departure of Trumper for the United States and G. for Trinidad—a more lucrative position outside the island. In other words, education becomes a process of literal alienation, taking students from the village and exporting them, like the material resources of the islands, elsewhere.

The school ceremony of the Queen's birthday celebrated shortly after G. tells us that his birthday was not an occasion for celebration consolidates the disparate process of colonial education. The narrator, in an ironic presentation of the procedures, emphasizes the ideological force of colonial pageantry that manipulates the colonized natives to celebrate Empire Day, an event that requires them to commemorate their own conquest. "There were small flags and big flags, round flags and square flags, flags with sticks and flags without sticks, and flags that wore the faces of kings and princes, ships, thrones and empires. . . . The children . . . seemed to see a mystery that was its own revelation, and there was, therefore, no need to ask questions" (36–37). The identity of the children is thus "interpellated," to use another Althusserian term, through the centrality of the distant metropolis and absent queen, both of whom are invisible. The lack of cognizance of these dominant "Subjects" makes little difference to their power, which is perhaps all the more effective in the haziness of the "recognition" that Althusser marks as a fundamental category of ideological interpellation. The face on the coin that stimulates so much debate between the boys in the classroom operates like a divine presence, asserting the illusory reality of the empire and British history and the unreal status of native history in the colonial classroom. A curriculum that ignores slavery but foregrounds the Battle of Hastings and William the Conqueror eventually constructs subjects who spend much time wondering which one of Britain's kings the face on the coin represents, even as it deprives the children of an active sense of their own environment. G.'s passage to high school aggravates the process of alienation, leading him to confess that his schooling was making the village fade into the background.

The school in any culture functions as an instrument for producing intellectuals whose formation is influenced by and, in turn, influences specific historical conditions. Education offers conceptions of history, culture, and identity that socialize intellectuals to mediate social and political functions in any given society. Ideally, education should involve a process of getting to know oneself through an ongoing relationship with the past, to be "plunged into history and [acquire] a historicising understanding of the world and of life," as Antonio Gramsci puts it.[18] But in the colonial system, education may also conversely involve a process of forgetting one's past and accepting the dominant positioning of one's place in the "World's History." When the process instantiates a sense of inferiority and shame and justifies the presence of the colonizers by parroting their assertion of moral and cultural superiority, colonial education consolidates colonial rule. What is at stake here is just how historiography affects history itself, since the assumption is that an active sense of one's history (narrative) is essential to activating one's history (praxis). I do not think that the process of colonial education wiped out all sense of agency on the part of the students. In spite of the focus on the negative aspects of colonial education in *In the Castle*, the alert curiosity and questioning among the schoolboys, their constant disregard for school and village authorities, indeed, the more active sense of rebellion among them show the reverse effects of their education. But the structures of colonial education were certainly inequitable, reproducing the systemic inequalities between England and the islands.

The academic premise that history and civilization were exclusive to the West was reflected not only in what the West Indian students studied—classical languages like Greek and Latin—but also in what they did not—Amerindian, African, and Asian cultures. The curriculum set by the Cambridge syndicate emphasized examinations rather than critical thinking, and the peripheral role that the colony played was sustained by the external examiners who judged the results of the reading they organized. Although what was taught in the schools, amid all the farce of Empire Day celebrations, gave centrality to the Great Tradition of English literature and culture, the students' participation could be only secondhand. Like the villagers in G.'s community, they were merely spectators vicariously and vaguely experiencing the achievements of an alien culture. Education itself, formulated on these lines, was regarded as an exhibit for display, a stepladder to the civil services, or a passport to England if one was fortunate enough to win the competitive island scholarships: as Lamming puts it, "something *to have,* but not *to use.*"[19] The consequences of the individualistic profit-oriented system become clear in *In the Castle* when Slime uses his educational background to negotiate with the landlord and deprive the villagers of their land. While the villagers respectfully attribute a great deal of power to education, they are themselves ironically gulled by the one educated leader they believe will use this power to help them.

Treachery of Slime's kind is only one of the reasons for the lack of concrete action among the villagers, who are perhaps too dependent on middle-class intellectuals in the novel and who rather naively, in Lamming's scheme of relationships, expect solidarity on racial lines. For other middle-class intellectuals, the educational process, as G. reveals, made it difficult to negotiate the binary worlds it set up. Immersed as he was in the national culture and history of the British intellectual, the "National Question" of the West Indies, C. L. R. James confesses, receded, like G.'s village, into the distance. James says, in *Beyond a Boundary,* "It was only long years after that I understood the limitation on spirit, vision and self-respect which was imposed on us by the fact that our masters, our curriculum, our code of morals, *everything* began from the basis that Britain was the source of all light and leading, and our business was to admire, wonder, imitate, learn. . . ."[20] But James, like Lamming, was to re-educate himself about the myth of England during his stay in England and his long exile from the islands. This intellectual crisis was to stimulate narrative production in a way that led writers in the West Indies "to speak for" themselves "in the modern world," as James claims, even before they left the islands. In the area of historical research, the goal was to correct the history of the colonies that had been obscured or distorted by Eurocentric versions. We cannot forget, of course, that while Lamming and James would like to see themselves as representatives of the lower classes, many of the intellectuals who were speaking for those "down below," had moved, by virtue of their education, to another class position. But it is certainly significant that there was a felt need to foreground at this time the traditionally overlooked proletariat and peasantry.

In "Proletarian or Revolutionary Literature: C. L. R. James and the Politics of the Trinidadian Renaissance," Hazel Carby stresses the need to contextualize internationally the events of the thirties.[21] Carby's approach in this article is politically relevant since her intention is not to universalize but to counter the reductive and isolationist studies of these events as merely local uprisings. It is important to remember that the skewed production that manufactured the intellectual in the colonies is not a thing of the past now that the colonies have achieved independence. Our reading of past events is still threatened by the cultural hegemony of Euro-American ideologies, making it essential, Carby cautions us, to look beyond the easily available, sanitized versions of the events of the thirties.

But Carby also argues that the renaissance of the thirties is directly indebted to the Russian Revolution and the Communist debates about literature during the twenties. Citing the "Resolution of the First All-Union Conference of Proletarian Writers" (1925), she notes that the terms and conditions of proletarian literature set out at the conference affected not just Europe and the United States but also the Caribbean. Lenin and Trotsky's recognition of literature as a cultural weapon and its role in mediating the relationship between formally educated intellectuals and peasants and workers was shared by West Indian writers who were interested in creating an indigenous literature that would take into account the lives of ordinary people. The particularly crucial intervention of creative writing in the area traditionally reserved for historians and sociologists becomes apparent in light of the fact that, in some cases, West Indian history was not introduced into the secondary school curriculum until 1939.

Creative writing, especially in the fifties, was similarly influenced by the imperative to present anticolonial critiques. Lamming's belief that the West Indian novel has largely focused on peasant life was to have important implications for a reconsideration of historical narratives as well. Just as James perceived the activities of the slaves in Haiti differently from the dominant view that expressed outrage and horror rather than praise or understanding, Lamming makes the point that West Indian fiction did indeed contribute to a more sympathetic consideration of the West Indian peasant, who "became, through the novelist's eye, a living existence, living in silence and joy and fear, involved in riot and carnival."[22] However, as I said earlier, we cannot ignore the differences in class position of those who actually claimed to speak and those they claimed to speak for.

In *In the Castle,* Trumper returns from the United States to the village with a new race consciousness that allows him to read the class struggle between the white landlord and the black workers and peasants more militantly than G., who has never left the island. The developmental process of insights into racism is rather problematic here because it suggests that those who have left the islands were somehow more radicalized. But Lamming's conviction about the brutal visibility of racism in the United States may have something to do with the way he presents Trumper's return. Moreover, the binary opposition between Trumper and G. is sharper than any rigid distinction between the former and the shoemaker's group, which discusses Marcus Garvey and the politics of race long before Trumper is old enough to leave the island. Trumper's use of Paul Robeson's spiritual, "Let My People Go," and his lectures on history, politics, and the identity of the "Negro" locate the specific site of Creighton's village within the larger context that I have just discussed. It seems that the various boundaries of the village will not prevent events elsewhere from seeping in: the strikes, the riots, World War II, immigrant politics, and the increasing U.S. presence in the Caribbean are mentioned briefly at the end of the novel. Lamming himself says that the deliberate historicizing of village life in particular and Barbadian politics in general was meant to oppose the generally held view that they were "very ordered, very conventional, very conservative."[23] But the riots and strikes in Barbados proved that the villages were not unaffected backwaters; the ripples spread both toward and away from this apparently remote and idyllic island.

In *In the Castle,* the villagers' representation of the fighting "coming" to the village seems to confer agency on the urban workers and obscures the fact that the strikes are initiated by the villagers as well, many of whom form the landless proletariat working in the shipping company owned by the Creightons. Although the 1937 riots enter the village scene dramatically in the novel, Lamming, less interested here in historical documentation than in the actions of the characters, only hints at the background to the strikes and riots that spread across the West Indian islands. The economic and political crises that preceded the strikes made conditions ripe for the revolutionary impetus of decolonization. The aftermath of World War I and competition in the sugar markets sharply depressed sugar prices. Rising unemployment, low wages, and the tightening of monopoly capital when the landowners took over shipping added to the pressure on the landless peasantry and urban workers. Increased dependence on imports, the Great Crash of 1929 and the ten-year depression that followed, and the 1924 Immigration or Quota Act that restricted British West Indians from the safety valve of emigration to the United States created more problems. These, along with alternating hurricanes and droughts, brought the islands to a boiling point. To make things worse, the colonial authorities showed no interest in ameliorating conditions in the colonies, apart from initiating lackluster committees and reports. Lamming's depiction of the unidentifiable royal face on the coin is an accurate representation of unreachable authorities—absentee capital and metropolitan control— who did not have to render accounts, at least not until the riots made themselves felt.

Early in 1935, a strike by agricultural laborers in St. Kitts was followed by strikes in Trinidad oilfields, and then in British Guiana, St. Vincent, and St. Lucia. In 1937, strikes and revolts spread in an igniting chain across Trinidad, Barbados, British Guiana, St. Lucia, and Jamaica. In March 1937, Clement Payne, a friend of Uriah Butler, who, along with Captain Cipriani in Trinidad and Alexander Bustamante and Norman Manley in Jamaica, was agitating for labor reforms, arrived in Barbados. He rapidly emerged as the leader of the working class, making connections between "race relations, black cultural suppression, the Pan-American nature of Garveyism, and Italian aggression towards

Ethiopia."[24] His fiery speeches were welcomed by his peasant and working-class audiences, but created unease among the colonial authorities. Seeking an excuse to expel him from the island, they accused him of entering Barbados on false pretenses. Although Payne was Barbadian in ancestry, he had not been born on the island. A minor technicality was turned into a major crime, as the authorities exploited the borders they had established between island nations and disregarded genealogy in order to rid themselves of Payne.

Payne's trial was attended by huge crowds, who gathered outside the courtroom to follow the proceedings. Convicted and fined ten pounds, Payne led a procession to the Governor's mansion to protest the sentence. Just as in the case of the Morant Bay rebellion of 1865, the authorities' refusal to speak to the people triggered the violence that was to follow. It seemed that the crowd would not tolerate silence any longer. Payne and a number of others were arrested. Although the Court of Appeals overturned his conviction, Payne was secretly deported without the knowledge of his supporters. The crowds at the wharf awaiting Payne's arrival from prison were infuriated when finally told about the deportation, and they expressed their anger in riots. When the news spread to the villages, the people there began to loot shops and raid potato fields, a tactic historically employed during particularly desperate periods of starvation. In the police firing that followed, fourteen died, forty-seven were wounded, and hundreds were arrested.[25]

Lamming's representation of the riots makes no mention of Payne, a significant omission given Lamming's interest in the issue of leadership, which he discusses at length in his later novel, *Of Age and Innocence*, where he more overtly shows the influence of the Payne trial. The forces behind the riots are the rural proletariat and the urban dockworkers, led by Slime and some politicians who quickly distance themselves, as several Barbadian leaders did, when the riots begin. The retelling of the story of the violence allows Payne to disappear as the immediate cause, emphasizing the long-standing grievances of the working class as a whole and their own control over their actions.

When consciousness of their reification asserts itself, the return to humanity on the part of the colonized is initiated through "absolute" violence, predicts Fanon.[26] It is also a process from the bottom up, he believes, contrary to all the claims of the nationalist leadership of having "won" independence for the people. Although one may quibble with Fanon's apotheosis of violence, and with the apotheosis of Fanon himself in postcolonial theories, decolonizing movements have generally followed his teleology of action. Fanon's schematization of apparently "random and senseless acts of violence" takes on the attributes of a ritualistic but confusing ceremony, an elaborately picturesque sequence of events in which the repressed anger of the natives simmers until a particular moment and then erupts in explosive violence. Lamming's novel runs remarkably parallel to Fanon's later theorization.

In *In the Castle*, the carefully constructed borders of the village are shifted by more than the storm. The apparently disconnected sequence of events that leads to the riots and the attempted murder of the landlord can, in fact, be traced through the erosion of the borders, first evident in the villagers' surreptitious surveillance of the landlord's everyday life. The actual "invasion" of the grounds by G., Boy Blue, and Trumper is construed as a threat by the landlord, who spreads the story that the boys had attempted to rape his daughter, a story she herself fabricates in order to disguise her clandestine meeting with a sailor. The change in the hierarchy that Creighton senses from that moment of trespass hints at the barely controlled unrest that will literally enter the village when the city workers stalk the landlord and attempt to kill him. The atmosphere of violence that Fanon describes is a short step away from explosion: "the guns go off by themselves, for nerves are jangled, fear reigns and everyone is trigger-happy."[27]

The violence finally depicted in the strikes in *In the Castle* is an equally unstable moment of disruption as it challenges the construction of the established and transparent social fabric. In a brilliant, tense exposition of the strikes and riots in the city, Lamming renders ambivalent and unknowable, even unseeable, the performance of revolution. The villagers who have not gone into the city get their information in jagged and incoherent patches, from a delirious boy and a drunk old woman, the accidental witnesses to the riots in the city:

> They [the villagers] waited, and later all the windows were pushed open again. Trumper came running through the road as Bob had done. He stopped now and again to say what he had seen, but the people couldn't understand because he never waited long enough to explain. Some heard about bottles, and others heard about stones, and there was some mention of shooting. If they had all got together, each putting his bit with the other's, they might have

been able to make a story, but they had to remain with the fragments. (194)

The following day the newspapers may collect those fragments, the villagers may compare their versions, and something more complete
might be put together. But in the demonstration of the riots as they take
place, Lamming shows the distinction between history as event and
history as narrative, or historiography. In his own account, what comes
through is not a linear, organized ordering of events, not a cause-and-
effect teleology, but disorderly, panicked scraps of information and
rumor split by the limitations of both individual vision and voice.

The exasperation and confusion of the villagers not participating
in the riots, the unpreparedness of the police force, the inadequacy of
politicians who watch helplessly as events go beyond their control, and
finally, the spontaneous and exuberant chain of working-class violence
on the official "monuments" of the colonial authorities and merchants
transform the riots into a carnivalesque scene, a gripping but confusing
melee of events and images. While the text itself makes no reference to
carnival in the account of the riots—unlike *Season of Adventure*, where
the mass demonstration is compared to a carnival—the festivity of the
riots in the city certainly suggests such a connection. The rowdy role
playing and the transgression of everyday boundaries allowed through
the license of the carnival temporarily suspends class and race privileges, since the tensions caused by the latter do not really disappear.
Instead, they are either held in abeyance or perhaps even displayed
through competing and conflicting carnival rites/riots. "The damage
took a strange form," says the narrator. "Cars were overturned, and the
bread vans making the early deliveries were stopped, emptied and
turned on one side in the gutters. Some of the men ate the loaves and
others used them as weapons to throw at the police" (*Castle*, 200).

While the riots in *In the Castle* are played out in a carnivalesque
mode, an important distinction between the riots and the carnival
needs underlining. On the one hand, the "madness" of the carnival is
within limits sanctioned, even mandated, by civil society and the state,
both of which (especially with an eye on the tourists) tolerate and, in
many cases, enjoy the annual interruption in regular life and regulated
system. The carnival discontinues the usual flow of city life and disrupts everyday activities within the relaxed rules that are specially
arranged for its performance. The riots, on the other hand, are unsanc-

tioned and illegal. Official and public response is framed through the rhetoric of toughness and intolerance: "the rioters will be caught and penalized"; "we will not tolerate any threat to law and order." The "celebration" of the riots, the breaking of boundaries, the violent challenge to the normative and established paradigms of social formations are therefore all fraught with peril. Although the carnival has also been criticized in various ways as vulgar, wasteful, and depraved, the profanity of riots operates far outside the realm of state and public tolerance. The text they present is usually met with utter incomprehension and hostility.

But riots are a language that various authorities are increasingly forced to confront and understand. The broken glass, looted and burned buildings, and glaring headlines deliberately "strike" us as disruptions in our usual patterns of life and bring to the surface what has long been ignored. The abuse to the social body and the evacuation of economic content tear down the facade of existing structures of subordination to reveal starkly the "inner city," the rotting core that such structures generate and conceal. The recent L.A. riots and the Chicago riots were not just expressions, respectively, of protest against the legally endorsed beating of a black man (Rodney King) by police officers or of a carnivalesque celebration of the 1992 NBA championship; they also brought to the forefront the economic need and social neglect that characterize the underprivileged areas of the cities.

The riots in *In the Castle* represent not so much a return of the repressed as the repressed made visible in a deliberately jarring manner. The accepted way of life in the city circumscribes most black people within rigidly drawn boundaries: those who serve, those who live in dilapidated shacks, those who have no right to the power and privileges available to people with skins of lighter shades. In *In the Castle*, the destruction of buildings, the attacks on the police, and the brief reversal of power relationships are all ruptures in the unwrinkled and orderly continuum of the class-and-race hierarchy that Creighton's personal history had initially endorsed as natural and inexorable. During the riots, there is "neither buying nor selling." The workers, in not allowing business as usual, manifest in unauthorized ways their invisible labor power. The narrator stresses the fact that there is no theft, although commodities are destroyed or scattered. Show windows of stores are smashed, silk and satin are trampled over, money is left untouched, loaves of bread from delivery vans are thrown at the police. The irreverence to and dysfunctionality of items of value, the contempt for capital, the disrespect to embodiments of colonial authority form a disjunctive and abnormal text that opposes and overturns the school ceremony on Empire Day. Here we have a carnivalesque mockery and decrowning of the king and a reversal of roles.

In one cameo of the multiple events, a worker/producer dons an evening suit in a store (the narrator overlooks this particular "theft") and assumes the role of uninvited consumer. In the confrontation that follows with the store walker, another reversal occurs in which the latter is forced into an ingratiating servitude:

> The worker simply asked him [the store walker] to stand in a corner and let him see what he looked like as an honest hard-working man. The store-walker obeyed, and in fright asked the worker whether he mightn't do other things an honest working man would do. The worker agreed, and the store walker set about shining the shoes and brushing the evening suit which the worker was wearing. The worker wrenched [*sic*] him in the ribs and told him that wasn't what an honest man did. The store walker shivered and tried to scrub the floor with his naked hand. The worker watched him with contempt and walked out to continue the fight in the evening suit. (200–201)

The store walker's response is clouded not just by fear, but by an almost complete lack of awareness of the complex range of labor performed by "honest hard-working" men. He imitates, therefore, his own stereotypical perception of what all workers ought to be doing: shoe shining and floor scrubbing.

Significantly, one structure of relationships stays in place. A female cashier is assaulted by the rioting men, whose sexual aggression targets her as one more symbol of everything that should be attacked (200). In this episode there is no reversal of roles; instead it is business as usual in the everyday politics of gender. Given that the world of the novel deals largely with the packed canvas of the village, the adolescent, emergent male perspective is complicated by other voices and characters, making it a fictional autobiography that goes beyond the individual. Still, to call the village a "collective character," as Lamming does, is to ignore the gender divisions, to use one example, within the community.[28] Although the women are not dominant characters, they are by no means unobtrusive. G.'s mother, for instance, represents as a single parent a common predicament in the Caribbean, where many of the men have migrated elsewhere or have otherwise been absentee fathers. In the dialogue between the schoolboys, mothers are perceived as "softer" than fathers, though how this stereotype holds, considering the frequent thrashings meted out by their mothers and vividly described in the novel, is intriguing. G.'s mother continues to have a strong influence on her son, and he follows the path her ambitions set for him, although she herself is yet to benefit from the advantages of his education. The issue of female education is not the primary concern here.[29] In this novel, the process of male individuation, culminating in the riots, is given more emphasis.

Trumper's advice to "act as you should" involves a consciousness of agency, something he had lacked as a child growing up within the confines of the village. In a conversation with the other boys, he, as a youngster, believes that the cyclical and unchanging rhythms of village life will never cease: "Everything's all right, 'tis the same yesterday an' today an' tomorrow an' forever as they says in the Bible" (120). In an earlier conversation between the schoolboys, after a severe and unjust beating by the head teacher has traumatized the children, the Fourth Boy announces amidst general approbation, "We going to make hist'ry. I always want to make some hist'ry" (48). The sudden shift in genre from prose to dramatic dialogue suggests the possibility of action, but also deflates it in the various conversations between the schoolchildren, who have little sense of their own history and only a hazy idea of the English one. Years later, Trumper reads village events in a different light, more aware of their historical significance. Contrary to his initial reading of the village as ahistorical, he senses, like the Fourth Boy, that history can be made in a village, too.

Not surprisingly, the need to make history foreshadows Fanon's scheme of inevitable violence. The desire on the part of the boys to stone the headmaster forecasts the later eruption of the strikes and riots. Both Trumper and the shoemaker assert that times are changing, implying the end of empire. Indeed, in spite of Trumper's doubts even as a child, he perceptively charts what Fanon would call the sudden emergence of revolution. "A thing go off in yuh head pop pop, an' you's a different man," he says (143). But unlike Fanon's conception of apocalyptic revolution, the novel makes the riots fade out, unable to keep up the momentum of the initial "pop pop."

The extended chase by the urban workers who enter the village to stalk and kill Creighton illustrates the deflation of the crisis. The reader is able to observe the hunt from a number of perspectives: the terrified villagers, who have mixed feelings about city people on their turf; the purposeful and seething workers, who are determined to make the landlord pay for Po's death; and Creighton himself, pale, sickly, and very vulnerable: "He walked shakily like a man exhausted and drunk . . . . His face was white as a pebble" (207). The apparently perfect Eden of the village with Creighton as the established divinity is exposed as a hoax when white mastery is now equated with a sickly pallor and targeted for attack.

Lamming himself, however, looks back on this passage with some regret. In his introduction, published thirty years after the original publication of the novel, Lamming regrets the cancellation of violence in the village when the workers' plan to kill Creighton is foiled by Slime's intervention. On rereading the passage, Lamming claims, he was "surprised by the mildness of its [the incident's] resolution." The novelist's desire on hindsight not only to reinvent the past—Lamming admits that no white man was killed in the riots—but also to rewrite his own novel comes from a need to fulfill in fiction what was not accomplished in history. To alter the incident such that the murder of the landlord is accomplished is not impelled, it seems, by an aesthetic desire for a more resolute and less anticlimactic plot. If anything, the controversial and bloodthirsty closure the writer later wishes to insert indicates a political desire to revise history itself. The death of the landlord, Lamming now believes, could have indicated the "symbolic end of a social order that deserved to be destroyed."[30] But neither the novel nor the history of what followed the riots provides the space for such neat messages.

As historical events suggest, the riots in themselves wrote an ambiguous text of revolution. They were certainly largely responsible for modernizing Barbados and other West Indian islands. Investigations of the riots such as the Moyne Commission Report initiated a number of changes. The government could no longer ignore the poverty and unemployment that led to the riots. Old-age pensions, legislation regarding workers' compensation, trade unions, and minimum wages began to be negotiated. The Barbados Progressive League was formed in 1938 to organize trade unions, to participate in elections, to aid emigration, and to promote land settlement. The Barbados Workers' Union, which Gordon Lewis called "the most remarkable of all West Indian trade unions," was formed in 1941.[31] Five years later, the Barbados Labor Party won the election and workers entered the political scene in an institutional forum.

Lamming's novel, however, does not conclude the riots on a note of euphoria celebrating the comradeship between leaders and masses. He himself believed that the revolution had been short-circuited by World War II and by the rise of the native middle class, both of which are depicted in the diffident conclusion. Although the thirties were characterized by what he calls the "politics in the street," the war "sabotaged" the radicalism of the riots, when domestic policies were suspended or repressed in order to focus energy on the war.[32] Lamming has a point here: although the Moyne Commission began their investigations in 1939, the report itself was initially suppressed because the large-scale bungling of colonial rule that it exposed was perceived as an unnecessary embarrassment in the context of the war. Just as the economic resources of the islands were depleted as the profits were pipelined into the mother country, the political struggles of the islands were stifled when most of the available human resources were needed for military service. Massive unemployment made the task of recruiting soldiers from the colonies an easy one. Any act of resistance toward the British metropolis during this period was construed as unpatriotic and seditious, although ironically, the large majority of West Indians were not allowed to vote by the same "motherland" for which they were expected to die.

Lamming also sees nothing to celebrate in the introduction of constitutional government and party politics because they reduced the masses to "spectators" and transferred the scene of action from the street to the parliament.[33] The large masses of workers and peasants were eventually preempted by the individual power struggles of party politicians and trade union leaders. As Fanon notes in his schematic outline of peasant resistance, the initial use of the countryside for strategic purposes is followed once again by an abandonment of rural issues for urban labor politics.[34] This is a pattern that played itself out, in spite of differences based on geographical, cultural, and historical factors, in several nationalist movements that first enlisted or relied on peasant revolt and then recentered "national" politics around the native metropolis.

The novelist's somber vision of the aftermath of the riots is captured in the novel's conclusion. The events that follow the riots in the novel do not lead one to infer that the new social order has in fact met the demands that led to the disturbances. Slime's entry into the colonial structures of power through his manipulation of the collective Friendly Society and Penny Bank sets the stage for the next act in the colonial drama—neocolonialism, the anticlimactic period of the struggles for independence. Slime's resignation as schoolteacher leads the villagers to believe that he will use his education to protect them. Indeed, his access to the villagers and their implicit trust in him are based primarily on his educational credentials, since education is a ticket to unquestionable respectability in the village. The grim reversal of their hopes, leading to the villagers being forced off the land and their houses being torn down, reinforces the sense of betrayal that the villagers feel and proves the irrelevance of customary ownership. The evacuations and demolitions are carried out in conjunction with a series of departures: the shoemaker disappears, the Old Man is sent to the almshouse, Trumper plans to return to the United States, and G. himself is preparing to leave for Trinidad on a teaching assignment.

Although the final vision in *In the Castle* is one of emptiness and loss, Lamming himself sees the novel as a tribute, not just to the villagers but also to the figure of Pa (borrowed from Papa Grandison, the novelist's godfather, who lost his house under similar circumstances). The writer sees his work as a productive attempt to "restore the castle where it belonged."[35] But Lamming's use of the novel as a site of cultural struggle and re-formation of village history only briefly mitigates the foreclosure of the land. After all, the villagers lose out precisely because they do not have the documentary authority that Slime's people possess; they can claim only traditional, oral ties to their land. As in the case of *Natives*, the lack of documentation marks monumental error, in this case the failure of the emerging nationalist revolution to gain independence for all. Some blank spaces in history will remain blank for the dispossessed. To the villagers, "There was something formidable, even sacred about a book. Only truth, it seemed, could be put in print" (92). Unfortunately, their truth about land ownership is denied validity not because it is unreliable, but because truth alone does not guarantee its authority. Only power can transfer it to print. In fact, as indicated in the villagers' belief, print then guarantees the status of truth. While Lamming's novel does fill in the "blank" of G.'s and the village's history, it obviously cannot substitute for the material fact of village displacement. In spite of Lamming's written testimony, the lack of printed attestation to the land on which the villagers have always worked remains in the novel a bitterly appropriate comment on their historical evacuation. While orality infuses the narrative structure and gives life to the written text, in the print culture of national belonging, it is not given the final say.

Chapter 4

Invented Histories: National Revolution in *Season of Adventure* and *Of Age and Innocence*

> This book is based upon facts of experience, and it is intended
> as an introduction to a dialogue between you and me. . . . Magic
> is permissible. Indeed, any method of presentation may be used.
> There is one exception. Don't tell lies. From time to time, the
> truth may go into hiding; but don't tell lies.
> —George Lamming, *The Pleasures of Exile*

> Such a mass of ignorance and falsehood has surrounded
> these islands for so many centuries that obvious truths sound
> like revelations.
> —C. L. R. James, Appendix to *The Black Jacobins*

John Isaac Shephard, the flawed messianic leader in Lamming's *Of Age and Innocence,* first exhorts the passengers he holds at gunpoint on an airplane from London to San Cristobal not to lie.[1] Lamming repeats the exhortation less threateningly but just as firmly in the poetic introduction to his collection of essays, *The Pleasures of Exile.*[2] Strikingly, neither the fictional character nor the author necessarily imply that not to lie will result in uncovering the factual truth. Shephard's threat is delivered during a maniacal fit in which he baffles the passengers with mystical poetry and yells insults at them. Seemingly the least rational of the many characters in Lamming's novels who go insane, Shephard, true to the type of the mad seer, provides one of the clearest insights about the status of reason and history in San Cristobal, Lamming's allegorical Caribbean island:

"San Cristobal, San Cristobal," he [Shephard] intoned. "You let rumor argue against reason in a voyage to San Cristobal which every race has reached and where the sea is silver and the mountains climb to the moon. You do not know San Cristobal, coming up by accident one morning from water, the tiny skull of a mountain top which was once asleep under the sea. . . . The past is all suspicion, now is an argument that will not end, and tomorrow for San Cristobal, tomorrow is like the air in your hand." (*Of Age*, 58)

Shephard finally claims to know San Cristobal, a knowledge he denies the others on the plane. But in offering the island as a "promise" rather than as a place, and in rendering past, present, and future equally unstable and open ended, his claim to knowledge is left as shaky as his grasp on reason.

Derek Walcott suggests ways in which one might read both Shephard's injunction and his subsequent creation of the myth of San Cristobal's emergence out of the water. In a lecture read to the University of Miami American Assembly on the United States and the Caribbean in April 1973, Walcott made what at first seems a startling claim. He said, "In the Caribbean history is irrelevant, not because it is not being created, or because it was sordid, but because it has never mattered; what has mattered is the loss of history, the amnesia of the races, what has become necessary is imagination, imagination as necessity, as invention."[3] Walcott's statement seems to echo the disavowal of native history asserted in colonialist historiography. His valorization of what stands in place of history—"imagination as necessity, as invention"— suggests, however, that he is refuting precisely the fact-finding enterprise of colonialist historiography that found only what amounted to "irrelevant" history in the West Indies. Generally, either the islands were claimed to be uninhabited or encounters with the natives were recorded without a sense of their belonging to history, except in the version meaningful to the colonialists. The usurpation of native land was accompanied by the repudiation of native narrative, a process of emptying out that caused "names, dates, circumstances, and truths to vanish"[4] when they applied to the Indians, slaves, and indentured servants. Such an act of prestidigitation demands the use of equally powerful magic to restore what was lost and to heal the amnesia.

Walcott's apparent dismissal of Caribbean history addresses not just the issue of historicity, but also of historiography itself. The writing of colonial history has not been devoid of mythification, of ideologies posing as timeless truths. But the polarity of truth and error has not much force in an area whose modern history was based on Columbus's monumental error of navigation. In the invention and imagination of Caribbean communities on the part of Caribbean writers, the rigidity of truth and lie is self-reflexively combated, not always in order to assert a final truth, but to choose a particular reading of the ways in which the Caribbean has been written into history. If nations, as Homi Bhabha argues, "like narratives, lose their origins in the myths of time," then all nations, it could be claimed, are subject to invention. What Lamming and Walcott are arguing is not that different from the more recent post-structuralist connections between language and the nation. To return to Bhabha, encountering "the nation *as it is written* displays a temporality of culture and social consciousness more in tune with the partial, overdetermined process by which textual meaning is produced through the articulation of difference in language."[5] In urging their audiences not to prevaricate, therefore, but subsequently inventing fictional and figural representations of the island's ontology, Lamming and Shephard both demonstrate that while foundational fictions may not be true, they are not necessarily lies.

The work of the imagination in the formation of national identities has generally been relegated to the sphere of false consciousness and irrationality.[6] In such readings, myth corresponds to falsehood and nationalisms are accused of being contradictorily and uselessly invested in a bourgeois, ethnocentric reversal to a mythic past. Lamming offers a counterperspective to such arguments in both *Season of Adventure* and *Of Age*. A conversation about a woman's personal humiliation in *Season* leads eventually to a discussion of historical memory and public shame: "Is like the island where you born. . . . It don't know how to find where it begin."[7] The antifoundationalism of this statement, however, provides the cue to invent such beginnings in order to come up with what Wilson Harris calls a "new corpus of sensibility" and a "new architecture of cultures" that can allow the Caribbean to take its place outside of the biases of colonial narratives.[8] Certainly such attempts may run the risk of being merely derivative, forever trapped within the confines of colonial epistemology, but this is where Walcott's use of necessity (as the mother of invention) might be particularly relevant. As Lamming illustrates in *Of Age,* when Mark is called upon to speak at a nationalist rally, at first he goes blank with stage fright. What launches him into speech is the recollection of the legend of the Tribe Boys and the Bandit Kings, a mythical retelling of the colonial encounter also allegorically presented in *Natives of My Person*. Mark locates the legend as a pedagogically and politically useful one because the resistance of the Tribe Boys teaches a lesson that ought to be learned in the context of the struggle for independence in San Cristobal. "The legend of the Tribe Boys is being enacted again in the history of this Movement for freedom," concludes Mark (*Of Age*, 173). "But here we can choose," he continues later. "And our choice is not complete until it becomes an act, for it is only action which can help us out of error . . . and only through the discovery of error that we may be able to define some truth" (174). As both *Season* and *Of Age* make clear, the work of the imagination can avoid romanticized stasis when it is put to everyday use in the daily life of the nation.

My own reconsideration of nation and imagination in *Season* focuses not on the visible, distinct, and homogeneous claims to ideological and geographic territoriality, but on Vodoun, a practice that emerged as a subculture in the colonial period. In spite of acceptance in some communities, Vodoun continues to enact in its underground rituals the fragmentation and elusiveness of a submerged diasporic history. George Lamming first witnessed the Vodoun Ceremony of the Souls during a visit to Haiti in 1956. He uses this experience in the first section of *Season*, titled "Arriving and Returning." Written six years before Barbados, Lamming's native island, achieved independence in 1966, the novel continues the allegory of the fictional, composite West Indian island called San Cristobal.

While the focus on black communities and Vodoun runs the risk of essentializing a hybrid and multivalenced culture as it exists today in the Caribbean, I will eventually argue that Vodoun is used in *Season* to recall and ritualize the memory of slavery as a specific passage in black history. Although Vodoun is a local Caribbean practice, it is significantly and predominantly connected with African rituals. Given its close ties with early slave revolt and racial consciousness in Haiti, the experience of Vodoun as a residual and an emergent subculture relocates traces of Africa in the elsewhere of the imagination.[9] My use of invention in the discussion of *Season* will be inflected by a variety of meanings as they come into play in the novel, such as, to discover obscured details, to fabricate a new history, to create a fictional story, to experiment ingeniously, or to produce something from nothing (as against finding or discovering something from what is already there). The associated sense of making an inventory, of compiling the traces of the past and giving it a clearer shape or form is also relevant in the putative formation of an Afro-Caribbean identity.

Lamming's use of Africa as a diasporic link figuratively represents the continent as a "zone of occult instability where the people dwell."[10] The amoeboid flexibility of the nation of San Cristobal corresponds to the mental as well as the material distribution of diaspora embodied in Paul Gilroy's emphasis on "circulation" and "mutation."[11] The slipperiness of the imagination explodes the totalizing boundaries of the existing nation, allowing it to travel across the rigidities of geopolitical mappings. Kamau Brathwaite captures the itinerary of one leg of diaspora in representing its course through the metaphor of seasonal winds blowing from the African coast into the Caribbean, bearing with them reminders of earlier winds and earlier currents that brought populations from African countries into the Caribbean islands.[12]

Specifically in the formation of the black diaspora, retrieving the past has involved its own difficulties because the degradation and violence that marked the forced scattering recorded a mangled heritage. The argument that the past is a wreck in Caribbean history has not been restricted to colonialist dismissals. Writers like Derek Walcott and V. S. Naipaul have also agreed that slave culture had little that was productive to offer. But while Walcott is impatient with any nostalgia for the past or a pre-Caribbean history, Naipaul's infamous remarks on the Caribbean islands are informed by his conviction that past events of slavery and indentured labor have irredeemably skewed the history of the West Indian diaspora and drained current history on the islands of any productive potential. Confessing that he was often awakened by nightmares that he was back in Trinidad (after nodding off by a fireside in English bedsitters), Naipaul explains that his fear of Trinidad was the result of his belief that the island was "unimportant, uncreative, cynical. . . . We lived in a society which denied itself heroes."[13]

Lamming believes that a similar shame directs the fear of Africa expressed by James Baldwin in *Notes of a Native Son* and offers an explanation for Baldwin's oppressive sense of past history:

> The backward glance is painful for it offers him [Baldwin] nothing but a vision of the bush, primitive, intractable, night-black in its inaccessibility. . . . We know what is meant by bush. It is the tom-

tom and the axe: the tom-tom always loud with noise, and the axe for ever suggestive of blood.[14]

Lamming's attempt to recuperate a more energizing vision of Africa in *Season* is not without a certain idealization, but it is also complicated by an awareness of the difficulty of maintaining a connecting thread when numerous historical factors have served to weaken it. Apart from the uprooting of clans with varying cultures and languages, once the slaves were relocated into plantation culture cohesive organization was difficult. Although her circumstances are different, Fola's ignorance of her real father's identity in *Season* has its historical roots in plantations where slaves constituted the master's chattel and not family units that allowed affiliation. Differences in ethnic and linguistic groups and labor functions also made slave unification a tenuous process.

Fola is initially presented as the passive subject of colonial education who, like the children in *In the Castle,* has been taught to repress the point of entry into San Cristobal during which all Africans were slaves before distinctions were made. Powell believes that "education an' class just twist that girl mouth right out o' shape," an indictment of Fola that is not contradicted in her preliminary reactions to the Vodoun ceremony she is brought to witness (*Season,* 21). But the ceremony becomes an educational process in itself, what she calls a "backward glance" that forces her to investigate her commonality with the women on the Reserve, lost, as Powell says, with the accretions of class and colonial education (49). However, as she herself realizes, the process of rediscovering origins is not an easy task for Fola. The racial community suggested at the *tonelle* is not as unified as it might seem. Powell might point to class and race as the issues, but his own misogynistic attitude toward Fola is consistently hostile even after she attempts to reconcile these differences.

Fanon's critique of "the return to Africa" move addresses not just its Eurocentric reiteration of a generalized continent, but also the teleological blunder it commits. It is not identification with but alienation from their national culture that makes the colonized, educated intellectuals grasp at the illusory "secure anchorage" of a Pan-African identity, Fanon argues. In spite of attempting to justify this desperate recourse to "mummified fragments," Fanon ultimately censures the invocation of a mythic Africa that he likens to a "cult or . . . religion."[15] Derek Walcott is equally dismissive of resuscitating dead gods, a metaphor he uses to critique what he considers a bankrupt intellectual romanticism that succeeds only in trivializing and commercializing the African connection.[16] It is interesting that both writers use the image of religion to reprove the invocation/evocation of Africa, because religion has been the sphere defined as premodern, traditional, and unscientific, all stereotypically associated with the African past before the intervention of the scientific, modern, secular West, especially once the West began to focus more on technology and less on Christianity as the sign of radical difference. And yet the meeting with dead gods, Lamming would argue, is not entirely outside the sphere of the living, the modern, the revolutionary. Nor is it simply a question of class and national alienation. Indeed, in the case of Vodoun, earlier largely a lower-class practice, the dead cannot speak except through the voices of the living, and very often they speak of matters that concern the material here and now. The ventriloquism does not make puppets out of living beings. The first section in *Season*, "Arriving and Returning," emphasizes dynamic circulation rather than stasis. Lamming's preference for the words *glance* and *presence* to indicate a return also carefully suggests temporality rather than timelessness, diffusion rather than rootedness. Rather than a definitive migration backward to Africa, the movement is metaphorical, strategic, and selective.

The Tropology of Africa

Since *Season* is ultimately concerned with the locality of the Caribbean, it is not with the tom-tom, but with its more contemporary Trinidadian (and now internationalized) counterpart, the music of the steel drums, that the novel opens. The novel itself is dedicated to Ghana, which Lamming had visited shortly after it had gained independence in 1956, the first African nation to do so. The Ceremony of the Souls that the drumbeats announce signals the tropological presence of Africa through rites of religion and celebration. As Lamming argues elsewhere, "If that presence be no more than a ghost, then it is like the ghost that haunted Hamlet, ordering memory and imagination to define and do their duty."[17] The directing role that the ghost plays in the Shakespearean drama, sternly exhorting Hamlet to seek retribution now that he has revealed the "true" history of his murder, makes Lamming's use of the ghost as a marker of African presence particularly appropriate.

Although the ceremony is concerned with recalling the spirits of the ancestors, the point of this resurrection is not nostalgia, sentimentality, or necrophilic obsession. The spirits are invoked with the specific purpose of guidance for the future based on, as Lamming says, "a full and honest report on their past relations with the living": an explanation of the familial and communal past and a public revelation of hidden secrets.[18]

The nonlinear narrative of Vodoun encodes the speech and image patterns peculiar to the enactment of possession: chants, songs, fragmented responses to questions, visions, swoons, dances, and so on. "Possession" resonates with a multiplicity of meanings within the colonial context that conditioned the birth of Vodoun. Fanon invokes two possible possessions in *The Wretched of the Earth:* one socioeconomic and political, the other psychoanalytic and therapeutic. In the first case, the native's "dreams of possession" embrace the affluent settler's space and stimulate the attempt to usurp the settler's ownership. The second use of possession is also marked by the defining role of the colonizers. "In under-developed countries," says Fanon, "the occult sphere is a sphere *belonging* to the community which is entirely under magical jurisdiction. By entangling myself in this [sphere] . . . I find the everlasting world which *belongs* to me."[19]

It is this "imaginary maze" that, according to Fanon, entraps one in the unproductive phase of possession. I use the word *unproductive* because while the repressed violence of the natives "is canalized by the emotional outlets of dance and possession by spirits,"[20] Fanon seems to find the expulsion of pent-up energy ultimately futile because the violent native grapples only with a shadow boxer. The sole positive aspect of possession in Fanon's account is minimized since it releases frustrations without always effecting a change in the social structure that is responsible for the native's condition. Further, Fanon's reference to the magical notion of "belonging" implies his critique of the fantastic world that allows the natives to delude themselves with the consolation of possessing at least one sphere that is beyond colonialist control. Their constant retreats to unreal locales apparently distract from the very real conditions of material dispossession in the colonial world.

Many cultural critics would object to Fanon's ambivalent attitude toward Vodoun as a significant political rite.[21] C. L. R. James draws the link between Vodoun as a conspiratorial, organizational political strategy and a creative, oppositional, cultural system. "In spite of all prohibitions, the slaves travelled miles to sing and dance and practise the rites and talk . . . and make their plans," he points out.[22] James reveals why the discomfort with Vodoun within the colonial framework was not restricted to its supposed lack of moral value. A more secular and material reason behind banning such practices was that they were often used to promote revolutionary struggle. The Haitian Revolution was believed, however mythically, to have been inaugurated by Boukman's Vodoun ceremony in 1791. These otherworldly rituals offered the possibility of more than spiritual salvation and physical or libidinal release to the devotees. Interwoven in the worship of ancestors was the promise of earthly liberation as well, especially through the magic of rituals that were said to protect the rebelling slaves from harm.

Interestingly, the ancestral souls were themselves dependent on the success of the Ceremony of the Souls—the truth being told and grievances redressed—for their own release from the watery purgatory, according to Lamming's rendering of Vodoun mythology, the preliminary stage of the soul's ascendance.[23] The frequent recurrence of the sea or water as location and image in Caribbean literature reminds us of the "long, wet hell of the Middle Passage,"[24] the historic slave past, the dissemination from one coast to another. Using an example of what he calls "the literature of reconnection," Brathwaite argues that Paule Marshall's description, in *The Chosen Place, the Timeless People,* of the sea as a raging burial ground for drowned slaves insists on recognizing "African presence in our society not as a static quality, but as root living, creative, and still part of the main."[25] Brathwaite's metaphor recapitulates Lamming's in charting not just a move outward, but its return inward in a continual chain. The emphasis on death and on the past underlines not so much the incarnate but the incorporeal grasp of African presence in the Caribbean. Paradoxically, the unmarked sites of watery genocide give witness to one of the areas of the absent presence of African ancestry.

Vodoun itself takes its name from *vodun,* the Dahomean word for spirit. The spirit of the corpse temporarily returning to the material enters through the crossroads between times, locations, and cultures. The *loa* themselves are a diasporic community of spirits, wandering from one group to another as their servitors summon them to appear. "When the gods left Africa, they taught their people how to live the epic of displacement," says Joan Dayan. She points out that the metaphor of mounting a horse, as the *loa* "rides" the servitor, underlines the mobility of possession, because the *"loa* are in the people not in the place."[26] Not only are the gods themselves multiple, they are also diverse in their manifestations across national and domestic affiliations, like the very people they both serve and are served by. In its circulation of diasporic traffic, Vodoun operates through a series of aporia, through moments of self-contradiction such as these: those who reenter are already departed, new birth emerges from painful partition, and the traditional ritual is also culturally contaminated as it adapts to everyday events.

Popular Western images of Vodoun rituals exploit their fetishization of the dead, indicated by the stereotypical representation in sensationalized horror films of the macabre and the undead.[27] But we should bear in mind Michael Taussig's cautions against an all-too-easy assumption that fantastic responses to nonfantastic realities are necessarily non-Western and backward. Far too many modern perceptions of reality are fetishized for us to target religious fetishism as a "primitive" mode that needs conversion to more rational thinking. Using Marx's characterization of market relations, Taussig draws attention to the ubiquitous presence of fetishes in a capitalistic, urban, industrialized, "advanced" society. And yet to the general public, the word *fetish* conjures up visions of primitive tribes and exotic figurines.

The critique of fetishism is based on the presupposition that qualities such as "life, autonomy, power, and even dominance" are drained from the animate to the inanimate in the process of exchange.[28] I want to argue that fetishism need not render the live subject passive or invisible. Folk superstition and magic have been criticized for the unreflected, uncritical beliefs they invoke and for the concrete acts of irrationality and injustice that such beliefs can generate. Much labor and time, it would seem, are expended on wasteful and wishful thinking. But religious and magical practices, like other ideologies, are not beliefs that lack value, although they might need constant critique and grounding in social relations. A fetishistic practice may cocoon the living in a fantasy world, but it may also utilize symbolic rituals and rites in order to engage productively in everyday life. The emergence of Vodoun within the context of slave revolt, its association with social practices such as oral communication and collective critique, and its carnivalesque rituals of singing, dancing, and drumming make it a unique personal and communal narrative grounded in, rather than dislocated from, a particular history.

The return to Africa in *Season* does not skip the history of slavery but uses it to *re-turn* to the point of literal and metaphorical entry into the Caribbean. As Crim says to the background of the drums, "perhaps contradiction help . . . but is the way you forget. Is not simple forget, is forget to remember" (16). Within the colonial system of education, what one was taught to forget was the arrival from Africa. Thus, the schoolboys in Lamming's *In the Castle* are hazy about slavery, and although they comically misunderstand British history, they are more grounded in the latter than in the former. When Lamming recounts his first impressions on arriving at Accra, school is what provides the "first shock of familiarity," as he watches the Boy Scouts rehearse the welcome of an English dignitary. But almost as soon as he recollects his childhood in the performance of the Ghanaian boys, the moment of connection is immediately and stridently ruptured when they begin to speak in Fanti and Ga: "The voices clashed like steel; and their hands were like batons conducting the wild cacophony of their argument."[29]

Lamming's attempt to commemorate the past in *Season* is similarly traumatic. Fola's return to an immediate as well as historical past is also initiated by wildness and cacophony, disconnection and confusion as she watches the *hounsi* (the female servitors) dance to the music of the drums. Her "fearful encounter with her forgotten self" at the *tonelle* where Fola witnesses the Ceremony of the Souls initially holds the terror and alienation pictured in one version of Lamming's backward glance. Her first reaction is to be repelled by the spirit possessions and by her unwilling sense of kinship with the dancing women. In spite of her attraction to the white history teacher, Charlot, who introduces her to the ritual, Fola is uneasily aware of her bond with the illiterate, lower-class, black women.

At the same time, Fola's shame proves that she has absorbed Charlot's history and shares his educational background. Ironically, she does not probe her fear of hypnosis and white rats to consider the implications of being possessed by a hostile and often alien culture and history. Her condition would therefore be more dangerous to the possessed women in the *tonelle*. The latter would regard Fola as a zombie whose physical power and psychic powerlessness emerge out of the slave context, since the living dead represent the dreaded condition of unfeeling servitude in a being whose soul has been stolen by the one now controlling it. Fola's and, by implication, the Republic's independence is meaningless because they are still controlled by the colonial paradigms of superior and inferior culture and history.

Conversely, Fola's later feverish delirium leads her to complete the connection between the dancing woman at the *tonelle*, Liza, and herself in the grip of a new possession:

> Her relation to the *tonelle* was *near* and more personal since the conditions of her life today, the conditions of Liza's life in this very moment, could recall a departure that that was near and tangible: the departure of those slaves who had started the serpent cult which the drums in their dumb eloquence had sought to resurrect. (93, emphasis in original)

Fola's very language begins to change from the "rules of college speech" to the "private dialect" that unite her and Liza, Crim, and Powell (91). It could be argued that the use of the drums as an African signifier is not much different from the colonialist stereotyping in which all Africans drummed, and all the drums sounded the same to the *bwanas*. But given the colonial conditions of production that define this novel, Lamming appropriates the drums in order to drill a different message about Africa. Rather than wincing at the thought of the drums, as she first does, Fola hears the difference more clearly now in spite of the distance between herself and the slaves, between herself and Liza. And the difference she hears, according to Lamming, is precisely what separates her from those colonialists who taught her how to wince in the first place. Fola's class status causes further distancing from those she now begins to see as part of her community.

In a scathing indictment of middle-class intellectuals who sell their talents and isolate themselves from the laboring classes, Lamming presents a topsy-turvy world in an informal talk he gave on Emancipation Day, 1986, to a village audience in Buxton, Guyana, which has a largely Afro-Guyanese population of slave ancestry. On the one hand there is the revolutionary history of the slaves and the laborers that continues to stay alive even if they are ignored or dead in official accounts. On the other hand there are the incipient "mercenaries," composed of the native middle class, which claims to be the most productive class even as it cuts itself off from that revolutionary consciousness. "It's the dead going through all the motions of living. The system of institutions—school, extension of school, church, law courts, all these institutions were in some way designed to turn the overwhelming majority of the population into zombies," Lamming concludes.[30] In his scheme, established and institutional forces discipline the subject into willing compliance with the state. Counterhegemonic potential, according to the novelist, lies in officially unrecognized sites whose very invisibility allows them to escape the fossilization of institutional politics and culture.

In *The Pleasures of Exile*, Lamming refers to Prospero's magic as one example of cultural power. The sheer spectacle of Prospero's conjuring freezes Ferdinand and Miranda into a captive audience. Lamming's analysis of Prospero's magic constitutes a discursive challenge to more than a literary drama. The tragic upheaval of the Middle Passage and the collective enslavement of the African peoples were believed to be the result of sorcery. Caliban, therefore, can be read as the zombie, the monster/slave "created" by Prospero. Hence Caliban must reject his interpellated identity and Prospero's invented history in order to enact his eventual resistance. It is not surprising that Lamming draws a parallel between Caliban's abortive revolt and Toussaint's more successful and collective "transformation of slaves" in the Haitian Revolution (1789–1804), during which the supposedly infallible superiority of the Europeans over black people was profoundly shaken.[31] *Season* is similarly engaged in a dialogic response to the Haitian Revolution, as well as to the genesis of Caribbean and Pan-Caribbean/African nationalisms. The reference to the Haitian ceremony and to C. L. R. James's *The Black Jacobins* in Lamming's discussion of *The Tempest* emphasizes the importance of folk rituals and revisionary history in the drama of revolution. Lamming's strong emphasis on the practice of Vodoun as an emancipatory project challenges the dominant perceptions of both Haiti and black populations as uncontrolled sites of gruesome exploits and anarchic misdirection.

Fola's visit to the *tonelle* ultimately revolutionizes her sense of her individual and collective history, and it provides the stimulus for concerted action. In fact, as I have suggested, her witnessing of Vodoun is an educative experience, reorienting her sense of historical placement. As Fola herself realizes, "she would make her own history" in the process of relearning her past (*Season*, 175). Fola, who is alienated from Agnes, her mother, needs at first to turn to the Reserve Boys for her revolutionary initiation, but later she emerges as more decisive than the Reserve Boys and intervenes at a critical moment to save them from police harrassment. Lamming problematically "creolizes" Fola's conception through the literal act of her mother's rape in order, it would seem, to represent the bastardized and violent parentage of the island. In a characteristically delayed disclosure much later in the novel, we are told that Agnes was seduced by a white man and then immediately raped by a black man after she was first caught masturbating in the forest by the bishop's nephew and then assaulted by the unidentified black man who witnessed the subsequent seduction (342–43). The racial divide is deliberately weighted against the black man, who is the rapist rather than the seducer, a difference that represents the colonial distinction between one (white) man's seduction and another (black) man's rape. In *Of Age,* in one of the intertextual slippages that occur in Lamming's novels, Bob catches his sister masturbating in the forest, is aroused, and worries over what might happen if a stranger was to come upon her (*Of Age,* 136). *Season* gives us an inkling of the fate Bob's sister escapes. The rape continues the problematic use of women as vulnerable symbols of colonial conflict, although its product, Fola, emerges as one of the strongest female characters in Lamming's novels.

Fola's eventual acceptance of folk traditions on the Reserve and her active bid to save the drums from extinction finally place her in direct opposition to the patriarchal, neocolonial elites represented by her stepfather, Piggot, the Chief Commissioner of Police and head of a committee in charge of "raising the moral tone of the country's name abroad" (*Season,* 102). Piggot's revulsion for the drummers and the Vodoun rituals mimics the language of the colonial administration in its anxiety to distance itself from the backward mentality of the masses. As Kamau Brathwaite sums up:

> The darkness of the night of ignorance, of voodoo drums and human sacrifice, of zombies, Congo gutturals, Dagon, Ogun, paingan women carnalized by gods. It was all of a piece, really, with what the Establishment thought of Africa and Africans in the New World; dumb, drumming, demoralized boyoes up to no good, inconsequential but needed.[32]

But the "moral" image alone is not the sole concern of Piggot and his lot. The Reserve on which the drummers and their families live and practice their rituals is also a valuable piece of real estate. It is therefore in Piggot's economic interest to ban the drums and rid the land of the lower-class practitioners whose rituals are tied to the land. The conflict between the native middle class and the people on the Reserve is, however, couched in the language of development and rationality, common strategies used during the period of colonization. The refusal of the lower classes to cooperate with the allegedly progressive, capitalist entrepreneurs by giving up their land and, with it, their practice, is translated into moral profligacy, while the profit-making agenda of Piggot and his lot is disguised as moral rectitude. The middle classes encourage an emphasis on folk or local culture only when it seems free of the risk of economic or political threat and when it can serve to invent a homogeneous nation. Since essentialist discourses such as negritude and Afrocentrism have often been appropriated by the alienated middle class to deemphasize class and gender issues, the novel's insistence on their explosive contiguity distances its reading of culture from the safer notion of ethnic or national similitude.

The practice of Vodoun inscribes the internal divisions within the nation even as it serves as a connecting link between diasporic communities. While the hegemonic interruption of the state reveals class tensions, some practices of Vodoun themselves dispel the rhetoric of community even within the same class when charms are used against members of a single group.[33] The recourse to the "modern" secular nation state of San Cristobal as a unifying, progressive, and mediating unit of diverse and competing cultures and countercultures is thus a tactic used to control fringes such as the Reserve.

Nation and Imagination: Invented Narratives

Lamming describes a similar tension in the opening lines of *The Pleasures of Exile*. The peasants in Haiti, threatened with imprisonment if caught participating in Vodoun ceremonies, play a game of hide-and-seek with the authorities that the slaves on plantations had played in different ways with the overseers and slave patrols. The elaborate and almost stylized rituals extend beyond the banned ceremony to include the police as unwitting participants in a street drama. Forced to move from the relatively secluded space of the *tonelle* due to the fear of a police raid, the peasants choose the anonymity and open space of the street. The *ververs*, the sacred symbols that indicate divine presence and initiate the opening of the ceremony, are quickly drawn in the dust.

When the police make a sudden swoop, Lamming goes on to say with unconcealed enjoyment, no arrests can be made because of the lack of evidence. Even as the police descend on the peasants, the latter arise to greet the law while their feet swiftly erase the marks in the dust. "But the moment the police depart, the signatures will be made again; the gods will return, and prayer will assume whatever needs those peasants whisper," concludes Lamming.[34]

The imaginative inventiveness of the peasants who inscribe their practice on available spaces and then remove those signs provides a new theory of writing and textuality that is literally deconstructed, literally under erasure. As Lamming points out, Prospero's magic is countered by the peasant "magic that vanishes and returns according to the contingencies of the moment."[35] The erasable but reappearing text refuses to be pinned down because the narrative and performative strategies of the dominated populations are rigorously monitored. Since disguising critiques of power is essential in social structures where open opposition can be life threatening, the rebellion is withdrawn to the outskirts of the legitimate space and inscribed in what James Scott calls the "hidden transcript."[36] The hidden transcript assumes many forms in Lamming's novel. The *tonelle,* for instance, serves as the "sequestered" space in which the lower classes engage in a celebration that is their own. The code language that the Reserve Boys use to baffle the police is another signifying system that cannot be read by those in power. The spirit possessions counter the condition of being "possessed" by the dominant groups by moving away, although only briefly and temporarily—a fact Scott's conception of the hidden transcript does not emphasize enough—from dominant social control.

But none of these rituals establishes the power of the masses institutionally. Like the marks in the dust, these subcultures are not solid and concrete as are the "monuments, cathedrals, important graves; the whole kingdom of names and faces which had been kept alive" for Charlot and his North American friends (*Season,* 73). Fola herself has no sustained or visible manifestations of historical agency and presence. Her confrontation with the Vodoun ritual serves as a jolting introduction to a history that, at the time the novel was written, remained largely screened from the public gaze. But Vodoun itself becomes an invented tradition that proposes its own "kingdom of names and faces."

The critical rupture with the past is precisely what gives the islands a unique culture and the possibility of renewed transformation and new beginnings. Therefore, even as connections are made with that point of rupture, it also serves as a point of entry into creative historiography. Just as Vodoun makes up its narrative as it goes along, often introducing new *loa* based on historical figures rather than gods, Fola's familial narrative is open to imaginative interpretation because it does not bear the weight of a long tradition. In the novel, justifying his "act of invention" in painting Fola's unknown father as he imagines him to be, Chiki thinks to himself, "Where nothing is known . . . it is easy to make invention credible" (*Season,* 278). The very nature of the gaps and spaces in West Indian history and, metonymically, in Fola's biographical knowledge, provide ample material for a "new" name and face. The impetus behind Fola's "season of adventure" is that she has been lied to about her familial past. Extending the lie to her larger history reveals the novel's oppositional stance to the lies told in an earlier, imperial adventure, colonization. Hence her "need to invent and leap beyond her past" is an intervention in two critical moments: in both colonial and neocolonial history.

Fola's strategic act of accusing her supposed father of the murder of the Vice President, Raymond, and her use of the painting as evidence of her father's return pushes a private exercise of the imagination into the public gaze of the nation, where rumor and reality, truth and falsehood, personal and communal merge together. The painting is reprinted and disseminated as copies are pasted in every public space in order to hunt down the culprit. So familiar does the painting become and so shared, at least in desire, is the act of murdering the hated Vice President, that men go to absurd lengths not to look like the invented face that stares out at them in mass produced posters. "Some people described how they would notice a change in the shape of a mouth or eyes, and got the feeling that their faces had started to take on the shape and expression of the assassin's" (308). Mimesis operates in reverse here as art begins to slide out of the canvas and imprint itself on reality. It also alters the course of events by allowing the real murderer from the Reserve to escape while the law sets off on a wild goose chase to find Fola's nonexistent father.

The multiple reproduction and repetition of constructed narratives (and of mass culture) also facilitates the second and more democratic Republic and saves both the Forest Reserve and the drums, a class-informed cultural expression in the novel. "People in Piggot class don' need the Bands . . . except for special celebration an' so, 'cause it have radio an' all class o' music box in their house. But the Bands is all we got," claims Jack, the brother of the famous drummer, Jack o' Lantern, who was killed in a police encounter over his drum (314). Piggot's resolve to silence the drums has its historical antecedent in colonial reactions to slave drumming, which was banned because it provided a communal framework for possible revolt. Part 2 of the novel is titled "The Revolt of the Drums," anthropomorphizing the drums in a manner similar to Lamming's use of the plow elsewhere.[37]

The steel drum was invented in the mid–twentieth century by black street gangs in Trinidad. They fashioned drums out of empty fifty-five-gallon oil barrels, transforming industrial waste into cultural expression in a process of magic, Lamming would say, that applies to West Indian culture in general. Waste itself has value in an impoverished world that continues to use or recycle what may be easily discarded in more prosperous worlds. Even the Vodoun gods, Dayan points out, have no objection to the miscellaneous leavings on their altars,[38] brought by a people who are as much of a cultural patchwork as their gifts of appeasement.

Lamming draws upon a history of silencing the subcultures, but goes on to present the explosive effects of musical practice among the masses. The attempt to ban all drumming in *Season* mobilizes the lower classes and leads to the massive demonstration against the corrupt First Republic. Once again Fola and Chiki, working, the narrator says, "like plantation slaves all night" (352), exploit print culture and improvise with laboring-class materials. Before it becomes official, the "national rumor" of the ban is pasted on the back of gin boxes and spread by fishermen and factory workers to organize a mass revolt. But what initiates the demonstration is Jack's vow to play the drum over his brother's grave. Great Gort goes a step further: he digs up Jack o' Lantern's drum from his grave and uses it to lead the march.

The drum, a vehicle of social protest and instrument of revolution, also functions in the novel as an agent of historicity. The act of retrieving the drum from the grave parallels the act of recalling the voice of an ancestor to guide the living. In this case, the beating of the drum at the head of the procession multiplies into the protesting "voices" of hundreds of household implements, such as kettles and spoons, which are beaten together as the sheer mass of people overwhelms the police. Artistic production is performed in conjunction with political praxis.

The polyphonous "cacophany" strategically uses elements of ritual religion and musical tradition; modern print culture and working-class labor; and African, Caribbean, and European influences in order to communicate, in both oral and written, verbal and nonverbal forms its mass protest. Although the possibility of a massacre is not entirely out of the question in a neocolonial nation, Lamming's construction of a successful revolution may have been inspired by C. L. R. James's account of the Haitian Revolution. Encouraged by the promise of liberation during Vodoun ceremonies, the slaves recklessly threw themselves into an initially unorganized armed struggle by fighting the formidably armed and organized French troops with "knives, picks, hoes, and sticks with iron points."[39] But as in the case of its historical predecessor, the revolution in the novel foreshadows not a future of unmitigated glory but, instead, a period of dashed hopes and continuing struggle. The novel's conclusion situates it in the transitory period between colonial and neocolonial governments, when the upbeat nationalism of the fifties, the economic optimism of the sixties, and the emergence of black consciousness as a politically viable movement were soon to be followed by fresh crises and uncertainties. In a conclusion reminiscent of *Of Age,* the novel ends with a weakened Great Gort concerned over Chiki's despair: the artist has lost his inspiration to paint because he can never match the energy of the drums. Like Thief, Gort "admits he is no prophet. He cannot name tomorrow" (367).

Since the Ceremony of the Souls demands the intervention of the past for future direction, the ceremony itself is a historical conduit for activist performance. In other words, history comes alive both in narrative and in performance through the folkloristic traditions of Vodoun, which serve an educational and, in the Gramscian sense, directive role. In the essay "On Education," Gramsci apparently approves of the child's insertion into state and civil society because it transforms his or her childlike "magical [folkloristic] conception" into a more modern, scientific worldview.[40] Clearly, Gramsci's Marxist valorization of the social discipline of work enables him to elevate the supposedly more adult progression into the rational over the stage of magic and superstition. But within the context of slave history, it was the magical world of the impossible and the superstitious that dispossessed populations turned to in order to seek respite from the drudgery of thankless and uncompensated labor. Music, too, played a role in alleviating the brutal conditions of labor even as its cadence was marked by brutality. The sugarcane laborers' often subversive chants were synchronized with the rhythm of the machete, the whiplash, and the overseer's abuse. But this is not to argue that the playful and artistic imagination was absolutely outside the realm of politics and labor. On the contrary, what needs to be emphasized is the inextricable connectedness of the imagined and the real, the spiritual and the material, the aesthetic and the political, the sacred and the profane.

In another, more receptive reading of the potential of folklore, Gramsci urges a serious approach to the "surviving mutilated and contaminated documents" of what amount to subaltern histories.[41] While Gramsci considers only intellectual scholarship on folklore in this case, Lamming's novel is invested in folklore as an active producer and not just as a narrator (or narrative document) of history. Although the irrational aspect of the imagination is clearly important in Lamming's project, since it counters constructions of the logical and the rational, the imagination is also valued as intellectual labor. Contrary to Gramsci's initial separation between folklore and education, in Lamming's use of it, folklore also functions pedagogically. Fola's witnessing of folk rituals initially distances her from the class she is merely observing at that point. But that encounter directs her later participation in the revolt, since it enables her to reconstitute herself in relation to a particular history. When Kofi James-Williams Baako[42] rebukes Chiki for using his people in his art without giving something back to that community, Lamming explores another possible meaning of return—an intellectual's return to the people not just as artistic but as activist participant. In Baako's definition, politics itself becomes art, an "art of the possible," and it is the responsibility of the intellectuals to open up the possibilities of the future to the community that inspires or nurtures them (324).[43]

The functional intellectual, however, is not always welcome in a community to which she does not belong. Fola's attempts to work with the people on the Reserve are met with hostility, and not just on the part of Powell. Fola believes that even Gort perceives her as an outsider, but that does not stop her from doing what she can to protect the Reserve. In the controversial "Author's Note," a section in which the authorial voice interrupts the fictional world of the narrative, the unidentified author uses the trope of the Lie and assumes responsibility for Powell's disappearance. The Lie, frequently referred to by Lamming in other works as well, is the distortion of colonial vision. In a passage that recalls Shephard's injunction not to lie, the unidentified author claims to have kept as close to the facts as possible. But his lack of knowledge about Powell's mysterious disappearance could extend to the history of San Cristobal as a whole. Just as Powell is interpreted in varying ways by the historians and analysts and novelists and poets, so too, it seems, can the island's narrative be available for multiple readings. "The present author doubts whether any writer, foreign or native to San Cristobal, historian or otherwise, is likely, at this time, to recover the truth," says the first-person narrator (330). This brief aside seems to be the foil to the main plot, which asserts alliance between the educated intellectuals and the Reserve rather than the division that alienates the author from Powell. Apparently ashamed of his distance from people like Powell, whom he claims as his half brother, the author confesses, "I don't think I should be far off the mark in describing myself as a peasant by birth, a colonial by education, and a traitor by instinct" (330). The nostalgic, guilt-ridden tone of this interruption is at odds with the directed endeavors of Chiki and Fola. Their return to the past, unlike the author's note, involves a more active retrieval of memory based not on regret and failure, but on a more inspired sense of the invented truths of their history.

The Return of the Intellectual

Lamming speaks of exile in many voices in *The Pleasures of Exile*. He is at once embittered, resigned, militant, critical, and angry. Exile becomes a precondition for the West Indian writer, out of place in "a society which is just not colonial by the actual circumstances of politics, but colonial in its very conception of its destiny."[44] Exile is also a mixed blessing for the writer who leaves the Caribbean, especially if the final destination is London, which provides distance from the frustrations of home space without quite severing its roots. But the ambiguous privilege of exile rapidly dissolves with the realization of irrelevance in England and increasing estrangement from the struggles at home. As in *Water With Berries*, Lamming posits such a moment of recognition as a timely one for return to the island in *Of Age and Innocence*. In fact, going to England helps accelerate the return by exploding the myth of England and the infallibility of the English. Paravecino's tirade to Crabbe says as much: "You can't pride yourself on liberty and deny them the experiment too. Nor can you go on enjoying the privileges of a lie at the expense of people who have discovered the lie" (168). Following the trajectory of the fleeing intellectual from *In the Castle of My Skin, Of Age,* written between *The Emigrants* and *Water With Berries,* returns the intellectual to the independence movement in San Cristobal. The connections between novels are often specific, as in Mark's recollections of the pebble and the crab (73) that recall G.'s encounters with them in *In the Castle.*[45] But while G. is directed by a sense of expectation regarding his impending departure for Trinidad, Mark's dominant feelings on the airplane to San Cristobal are of pessimistic and fearful gloom.

Mark unearths long-buried childhood memories on the island and regains some sense of belonging, but he continues to remain a largely negative character, with only a muted sense of expectation upon his return home after some twenty years away. Briefly energized by the struggle to take over the colonial state, he feels a momentary sense of direction when thrust into the midst of the daily political meetings. Lamming's notion of the purpose behind return after exile is made abundantly clear when Mark burns his biography of an eighteenth-century pirate and turns his attention to the task of rallying for Shephard, Singh, and Lee. Mark has no regrets: "each account can only be a fresh corpse which we assemble in order to dissect again. Nothing was lost when I burnt the last pages of the pirate's biography. I had only burnt a little corpse whose original I could never know" (*Of Age,* 107). If the emphasis in *Season* is on reviving the dead, Mark's determination to put the dead to rest does not contradict the writer's agenda in the former novel. The difference lies in the choice Lamming makes regarding resurrection for some and incineration for others. In reconstructing the nation's history, Lamming reverses the moment of forgetting and the moment of remembering. In Mark's gesture, the colonial focus "from the dreary pile of history" is burned in a replay of the burning of the canefields (107). In Fola's witnessing of a Vodoun ceremony, however, those that have been forgotten, her black ancestors, resurface to direct the season of her adventure.

But for Mark, there is no such adventure in store upon his return, which completes itself literally, but fails metaphorically. The locked-in interiority and the rather bemused reflections of G.'s diary are repeated in Mark's diary, the only form of writing he now maintains. Characterized by a taciturn unwillingness to communicate openly, either to his lover, Marcia, or to his English friends, Bill and Penelope, who accompany them to San Cristobal, Mark's almost total sense of isolation imprisons him in a silence broken only by his observations in his diary. Even these notes are not entirely successful and actually lead to Marcia's madness when she realizes, upon reading Mark's diary, how little he values her. While language has potentially liberating capacities, it can also wound. And while it may clarify and stimulate, especially in the oral tales of San Cristobal, the language of Mark's diary has little productive potential. As in Penelope's case, the revelations in Mark's diary are structured through a solipsistic, claustrophobic stream of consciousness.

Similar to Roger's reaction to his white wife in *Water With Berries*, Mark's increasing sense of commitment to the national struggle creates a distance from his white lover and friends, who are all perceived to be an embarrassment in the tense racial politics of the island. Although Bill, Penelope, Marcia, and Flagstead are, in spite of some qualms, largely sympathetic to universal franchise, they are all outsiders from England, isolated from the native white community that is largely reluctant to give up power and from the colored population that feels whites have for too long held the reins of government. Mark's increasing diffidence comes from a sense not that his memory has failed him, but rather that, like his friends, he too is an outsider, "out of touch" with San Cristobal after so many years of absence. As a result, he tries to distance himself from the English visitors, uneasily conscious of belonging neither with them nor with the residents of San Cristobal.

Shephard's return, on the other hand, immerses him immediately and directly in the movement for independence. In spite of his madness on the plane and a short stay in an asylum, he is welcomed back into the community as the messianic leader who will guide to victory the party, the People's Communal Movement, formed by himself, Singh, a former canecutter, and Lee, a retired schoolteacher. Lamming constructs an emerging nation united for the purpose of independence at the moment of universal franchise, but allows it to unravel even before the elections are held. The tensions and suspicions between racial and ethnic groups run too deep for any easy resolution. A combination of accidental occurrences, such as the fire at the asylum, and deliberate sabotage by Baboo, the Indian constable, eventually ring the death knell for nationalist leadership. Although Lamming focuses on intra-island conflicts, the dismantling of centralized politics is an uncanny foreshadowing of the fate of the Federation of the West Indies, which was formed in 1958, the year in which *Of Age* was published, and which swiftly collapsed in 1962. The novelist was a supporter of the Federation and shared James's Pan-Caribbean and black diasporic convictions, but the novel itself displays a deep skepticism, not just for a unified black consciousness movement, but also for the rhetoric of interracial harmony.

Interestingly, the novels that are set in England, *The Emigrants* and *Water With Berries,* do not present a federalist West Indian identity as an impossibility, but rather insist that a unified intranational identity would be the best resource against the English. Back home, however, the stakes are different. While *In the Castle* uses Barbados as an example of the disruption of race unification through class differences, *Of Age* seems to borrow from the racial troubles between Afro- and Indo-Caribbeans in Trinidad and Guyana. The leaders in the latter novel seem more committed than the treacherous Mr. Slime in the former novel, but Singh's double agent, Baboo, allows his ambition to see Singh at the helm to overcome Singh's own respect and deference to Shephard, and ultimately assassinates the black leader.

Although the dramatic dialogue between the voices during the trial of Bill and Mark, mistakenly held accountable for the murder of Shephard, deifies the latter, the narrative itself refuses to idealize the dead leader. Initially representing Shephard as driven to madness by the contingencies of colonialism and by the deceit of his white lover in England, Lamming later goes on to depict him as drunk with power and ambition. Shephard's delirious raving before a dazed Mark reveals the self-serving aggrandizement that, as Lamming implies, characterized the nationalist leaders who took over the independence movement. All the signs point to Shephard's similarity with the neocolonial leadership that assumed power through mass support and then rapidly proceeded, like Mr. Slime, to alienate itself from the people it claimed to have saved. *Of Age* predicts the future of many "people's" parties in Barbados, Guyana, Trinidad, and Grenada, which collapsed when the vanguardist leadership allowed its internal squabbles and egotistic struggles for power to betray the purpose of electoral politics.

Lamming indicates some of the inherent problems with nationalist leadership and warns about Shephard's obsession with power in his choice of the novel's epigraph, which quotes from Djuna Barnes's *Nightwood:* "A strong sense of identity makes a man feel he can do no wrong; too little accomplishes the same." Mark first picks up on the underlying instability behind Shephard's assurance but goes on to see it as a shared condition: "Can it be that Shephard has always been, in the past, afraid or ashamed to see himself? I ask this question of Shephard and at the same time I feel it is a question I have also put in silence to myself" (*Of Age*, 111). Shephard's precarious mental health is traced back to his youth, when, as a boy, Mark witnesses his strange behavior with chairs. Shephard addresses a bunch of chairs as if they were his subject population, and what might seem a boyish quirk assumes more serious dimensions in the light of his later reference to the significance of the chairs. In playacting with the silent furniture and adjuring these objects to obedience, Shephard may be psychologically compensating for his feeling of worthlessness in a colonial society (109). But Mark is right in sensing a shared loss of identity even as he is unnerved by what to him are Shephard's first indications of insanity, his continued inability to distinguish between the real and the make-believe.

Mark's empathy for Shephard comes from his own awareness of his racial difference in England. In spite of the fact that Marcia is presented largely as a victim of Mark's coldness and seems more warm than her lover, a brief moment in the plane gives away her own racial anxieties. Roaming idly over the passengers, Marcia's glance finally focuses on Mark, who becomes "an object situated there." The rest of the description as she runs her eyes over him identifies him through racialized biological markers, such as his skin and hair (34). Oblivious at this moment to the objectification in Marcia's gaze, Mark must nevertheless not be a stranger to the experience of being made to feel an object. Forever on trial with his body as witness and defendant, Mark flinches from the prosecuting eye, particularly potent in England. "And there are times when I have felt my presence utterly burnt up by the glance which another had given me," he confesses (112). His burning of the manuscript is a response to that memory as well.

Shephard's later reference to the chairs in an encounter with Penelope goes beyond Mark's hazy misgivings to articulate a theory of coming to consciousness. "But like the chair, I have played no part at all in the making of that meaning which others use to define me completely," he tells Penelope (203). Shephard uses this moment to excuse his behavior to Penelope on the plane when he launches into a long and vituperative curse. "Caliban's" curse is used against Penelope, who reminds Shephard of his destructive former lover in England. Ironically, while

Shephard bemoans his undifferentiated objectification in the colonial system, he seems to have no critical awareness of the problems involved in conflating one woman with another or in regarding his "flock" as a bunch of chairs open to manipulation. It is left to Penelope to make the connections between her own emerging lesbian identity and Shephard's use of the chair as a symbol of racial and class reification. Moved by Shephard's rhetoric, she recollects her thoughts when first coming to grips with her desire for Marcia. "The Negro, the homosexual, the Jew, the worker . . . he is a man, that is never denied, but he is not quite ready for definition until these reservations are stated, and it is the reservation which separates him from himself" (151). As in *The Emigrants*, the lesbian relationship is located within the related systems of difference, the lesbian cringing along with the others at the thought of being "branded" and isolated by the dominant culture. Here, too, however, as in *Water With Berries*, the main female characters are killed off, leaving only the conservative Ma Shephard as the sole survivor. Penelope's sense of the "in spite of," the "reservation" of difference that ultimately marks her is never resolved: she dies without ever telling Marcia of her love.

The conclusion to the novel is perhaps the bleakest of Lamming's many bleak endings, surpassing even *Water With Berries* in its overwhelming sense of failure and paralysis. As in other novels, Lamming uses the mechanized waterfront landscape to set the scene:

> Crows were collecting again over the iron shed, and the flies were busy round the wet entrails of fish stacked high on the coarse crocus bags. It was hot and the men were wet and rough. Far from the lethargy of this waterfront they heard a horn hoot, and the rails seemed to rock and scream under the spinning wheels. The flies dispersed in terror, and the crows fled reluctantly away. (*Of Age,* 385)

The sense of defeat moves from the insects and birds to the people themselves, as the various racial groups are weighed down in a stereotypical replay of colonial roles. The Indians look spiteful and secretive, the blacks seem "indolent" and "destructive," and the Chinese appear "severe" and "stoic" (385). As if to complete the humiliating turn of events, the army moves in and the island is put under curfew.

The narrative heaviness, more apparent here than in other novels by Lamming, is not, however, one of unmitigated paralysis. Neither age nor innocence, it is true, seems capable of emerging unscathed from colonial desolation. In fact, the errors of age infect the potential of innocence, until innocence becomes, as Thief says, a meaningless word in a world riven by guilt (370). In the very moment of justifying the value of nationalism, Mark is suddenly prey to intense anxieties about its expression in electoral politics:

> It was a strange and monstrous diversity of forms and noises which inhabited his mind. And amidst this natural corrosion he could hear voices announcing the crowd's wish to be ruled. Vote for the star. Vote for the donkey. Vote for the aeroplane. Vote for the knife. It was as though the voices existed in their own right, faceless and inhuman. And gradually they gave way to the cry of a kid, the petulant, despairing shriek of the new born. (175)

Certainly Mark need not be conflated with the author, but Mark's premonition is not irrelevant to the final frustration of hopes for democratic self rule amidst national differences. As in a significant number of postcolonial novels that equate emerging nationhood with infancy and childhood, the newly born nation here howls its inadequacies and fears as its birth is prematurely celebrated. Tomorrow, represented by the children and representing new hopes, is at first buoyantly anticipated by Thief when he envisages a color-blind future that will unite the Indians and blacks on the island. "See how Singh let Shephard lead, 'cause the blacks outnumber all, but the numbers don't matter no more, Baboo," says Thief, "an' we goin' join the same dream that wake with the Chinese too, an' any white who willing. 'Cause San Cristobal aint got no history but a people who collect in one place by some strange chance" (81). Ironically, Baboo destroys Thief's dream of a smiling future, and by the end of the novel, Thief grimly declines to comment on what the outcome of the events might be. "Tomorrow ain't got no name," is all he will say (394).

Still, Lamming reserves some hope for the younger generation. The engaging curiosity and independence asserted by the offspring of Singh and Lee (also given the same names), their black friend, Bob, and their white friend, Rowley, a recent addition to the group, lighten the powerlessness of the adult world they surpass in their mimicry. Beginning as a "satire" on the adult world around them, the secret society that they form rapidly gains an identity of its own. "It had made their age irrelevant, compared with the wasted experience of those who were so much older," observes the unnamed narrator (115). The transverse, temporal clock-and-calendar time of the nation is shifted to Benjamin's notion of "Messianic time, a simultaneity of past and future in an instantaneous present."[46] For reasons I will explain later, print culture and the conception of history as a separation between past and present is absent from the children's apprehension of the future nation. "Then child, boy and man all seem to happen together without distinction of years and time. Like how we moving here this morning to start something new," reflects Bob (116). This is not to relegate San Cristobal to the medieval "figuring of imagined reality [that] was overwhelmingly visual and aural,"[47] but to argue that the oral culture of the boys' world resists the inscribed versions of the colonial narrative by turning to the myths and legends absent in the writing of the colonial nation. The legend of the Tribe Boys helps the children "remember the faces of those who died" by resurrecting the period of early colonialism from the point of view of the colonized (27).

The children in *In the Castle* demonstrate Benedict Anderson's modern biography of the nation, taught as they are in school to revere the commonwealth of nations under the benevolent aegis of a Mother England and its distant royalty. In their slippery grasp of slavery, the deaths of their ancestors are not much matter for deliberation. The massive exhumation that Lamming undertakes, through Vodoun in *Season* and by means of the legend of the Tribe Boys in *Of Age*, forces a remembering of what has been forgotten in the colonial account. The emphasis on boys both in the earlier colonial encounter and its later reenactment, however, limits its devastation to fratricide and the reemergence to a fraternity, which leaves out women. Even though the boys learn of the legend from Ma Shephard, who functions as the folkloric voice, she, unlike them, is apparently unable to grasp the resistance embodied in the legend and disapproves of the burning of the canefields as needless destruction.

As in *Season*, Lamming's reconstruction of Caribbean mythology is markedly influenced by the Haitian Revolution, borrowing, for instance, the widespread burning of property by Haitian slaves who preferred to leave nothing behind for the French. But it also goes further back, to the early encounters with the Amerindians, who, unlike the more general Tribes in *Natives*, are gendered here as the Tribe Boys, a precolonial predecessor perhaps to the Boys on the Reserve in *Season*. The counterhegemonic potential of the memory of continual resistance to colonial invasion and settlement is apparent in the appropriation of the legend by Mark at a nationalist rally and by the children at the end of the novel. As in other retellings in Lamming's novels, though, the elemental, originary myths of the nation defy romanticization about glorious origins because of the terrible destruction they embody. As in the case of Vodoun, they bring the dead back to life, back into the present time of the nation through their invention, but they do not erase the circumstances of the genocide. In both novels, the inventions reach a politically sensitized audience, who make plans for action based on these accounts. In what has now become a commonplace in postcolonial literature, art and praxis are combined in a communal forum.

What are the life-giving possibilities of keeping track of the dead? One answer is provided by Alice Walker's determined pursuit of Zora Neale Hurston's unmarked grave in the Garden of Heavenly Rest, a segregated cemetery in Fort Pierce, Florida. Walker's determination to mark that particular spot is symbolic of her need to track down and record an obscured black "womanist" tradition in her collection of essays, *In Search of Our Mother's Gardens*.[48] The identified spot may have been mythical and may have had nothing to do with Hurston's remains. The factual materiality of the final resting spot of the body is as irrelevant as whether or not Boukman did conduct a Vodoun ceremony that initiated the Haitian Revolution. Henry Louis Gates Jr. notes that after being ignored by the American literati for years after her death, Hurston's reinstatement into the African-American literary tradition was significantly enabled by, among other black women writers, Walker's indebtedness to Hurston. "The excavation of buried life helped a new generation read Hurston again," he concludes.[49]

Lamming's use of the legend of the Tribe Boys in *Of Age* has a similar significance for the living, although in this case *womanism* is not a consideration. The three boys, Bob, Singh, and Lee, who represent the three major racial groups of the island, relate the story for a price. The story is thus transformed from aesthetic account to economic value, because, as the boys insist, the collective labor of the boys "make[s] a big history" (101) out of a little-known or silenced event, the struggle of the Higuet Indians against European invaders.[50] Although the legend combines the elements of myth and allegory, the story of the Tribe Boys is a historical one as well.

Borrowing much of Ma's account of the origins of the island, the boys continue the tale from where she stops with the wind, fire, and flood in their retelling of it to Marcia and Penelope. The Tribe Boys came to the island after its elemental beginnings, they claim, and lived in peace until the arrival of the Bandit Kings, clearly the colonizers. What follows is a recapitulation of the enslavement and, failing that, the extermination of the native Indians by the Europeans. Unable to withstand the armed might of the invaders, in spite of victories achieved through guerrilla warfare, the remaining Tribe Boys eventually gather at the top of the cliff of Mount Misery and leap to their deaths. The final scene in the novel where the boys are gathered over Rowley's grave in the cemetery on All Saint's Day underlines the significance of the dead in Lamming's novels. When Fola wanders through the cemetery in search of her origins, when she participates in what might seem a bizarre ritual involving the dead, the monuments of her history, Lamming implies, are built on the scores of people who have been annihilated since the grand moment of Columbus's discovery. It might have meant a "brave new world" and a new life for the subsequent settlers, but, as Lamming grimly reminds us, it came at a high cost. Recalling the various Amerindians, the Caribs, Tainos, Arawaks, and Ciboneyes (not all of whom lived in peace with each other, contrary to Lamming's revisionist account), as well as the later Maroons of Jamaica and the so-called Bush Negroes of Surinam, the legend maintains a line of guerrilla resistance in the Caribbean.

Lamming also revives the tradition of arson as a militant strategy in the Caribbean, particularly in the burning of the cane fields and of the monuments of colonial rule. The institutions of state force and consensus—the library, the church, and the constabulary—are at first presented as established sites with a long history. Marcia and Penelope's tour of San Cristobal directs them to these and other official landmarks: the statues of the seventeenth-century French colonialist settler, Louis de Ponge, and his English counterpart, Brummel. Evidence of French and British colonial power is presented through the statues, but undermined by the revelation that the great fire of San Cristobal has destroyed any documentation in the library. Penelope rightly indicates the hegemonic status of the statues and suggests, "If those powers had sufficient imagination . . . after they'd got what they wanted, they should have raised a statue to an unknown native of San Cristobal" (88). The possibility of paying tribute to an "unknown native" is, of course, remote given the priorities of the colonial powers, who were hardly likely to be grateful to the natives for giving them "what they wanted." But the several unknown natives who start the fires nevertheless have their revenge in the destruction of colonial documents that do not grant them any space. Instead, the legend of the Wild Fire ironically gains legitimacy by becoming, due to its devastation of plantation wealth and colonial historical records, "a text for teachers" (68).

The arson is repeated in the modern context of *Of Age* with particularly brutal effects. The accidental burning down of the asylum by one of the residents, leading to the deaths of Penelope, Marcia, and young Rowley, among others, is partly responsible for taking the anticipation out of the elections, leaving San Cristobal to feel it is under a "curse." In the mowing down of characters who could be considered guiltless, Lamming once again asserts, as he does in *Pleasures*, that "there are no degrees of innocence."[51] In one of the bitter ironies of the text, the lighter that causes the explosion was made in England and is given to Rowley as a gift by young Singh, who steals it from his father. The lighter is given as a sign of friendship and acceptance and also as a pledge to secrecy about the society into which Rowley is initiated. The exchange relation makes friendship with a white boy become the intrinsic value of the made-in-England lighter and is then located within the colonial capital-labor conflict of the power strike. During this strike, the shopkeepers, in support of the striking electrical workers, refuse to sell oil, which could substitute for electric power, to the perceived sympathizers of colonial rule. Clearly, Rowley's father, Crabbe, who is the Chief of Police, runs the Government Information Services, and has shares in Radio San Cristobal, is targeted for exclusion. The boys attempt to overcome the tensions between their warring fathers by secretly procuring oil for Crabbe, who they hope will purchase it and add to the funds of the secret society. Instead, through a series of coincidences, the two commodities, the lighter and the cans of oil in Crabbe's car, the markers of racial harmony in the new generation, the symbols of forgiveness between colonizer and colonized, meet in an explosive conflagration through the unwitting agency of a resident of the asylum. In a literal explosion of the secret of commodity capital and colonial guilt, the hidden social relations that the strike and demonstration at the asylum are intended to express are brought out in the open with calamitous results for much of the community. The arrival of the troops after Crabbe's murder and Singh's imprisonment dispels the pretense of liberal democracy promised in the elections as the repressive state mechanisms are forced to reveal themselves.

The folk wisdom expressed to Penelope at an earlier point in the novel by an unnamed man in the crowd continues to resonate in the novel's conclusion. "Everywhere, madam, is politics," he says succinctly (82). Apparently agreeing with James that Toussaint's failure lay in forgetting the masses after the Haitian Revolution, Lamming gives up on the leaders but clearly has not abandoned hope in the emergence of the national-popular. *Season* and *Of Age* offer diametrically opposing views regarding the success of alliances between classes. Different social elements are able to come together in one novel but fail to coordinate their interests in the other. The exchange in *Season* seems to succeed because no rigid distinctions are drawn between the intellectuals and the people. In *Of Age*, however, the movement is doomed to failure in the unproductive distance between the leaders and the people. The disarray in leadership does not entirely sap the collective will, even if it fragments it. The elections have been stalled, but new "candidates" emerge in less bureaucratic and more subversive ways. The narrator reports

> after nine days there hadn't been a single incident, and at night some of the troops would disguise [themselves] in civilian clothes to go whoring in the slums. It was then that they talked, and often the women repeated what they had heard. . . . Hatred was beginning to grow, collecting candidates like a plague. (394)

In the dissemination of carelessly dropped official information and the spread of talk and rumor, Lamming suggests that the revolt is not dead, merely lying in wait. But, as in many other novels, what tomorrow brings remains to be seen.

Conclusion

"We Are a Future They Must Learn"

"We haven't produced the women writers as yet. George Lamming tells me that he is waiting for the woman in the Caribbean to write a novel which will state the position of the Caribbean. Well, he is waiting for her. I am waiting for her too."[1] Thus speaks C. L. R. James in 1980, mystifyingly relegating women writers to a hazy future almost two decades after Sylvia Wynter had published *The Hills of Hebron*.

What makes the wait by Lamming, more than James, especially difficult to comprehend is that Wynter, who is also a lively literary critic, works in a black nationalist tradition similar to Lamming's. *The Hills*, in fact, expresses some of the same concerns as Lamming's *Season of Adventure* and *Of Age and Innocence*. Unlike *Season*, however, which stresses the revolutionary role of Vodoun, even if it ends with the humiliation and disorientation of the *houngan*, *The Hills* is less enthusiastic about the potential of religion. But Wynter is equally committed to a tradition of African-inspired and communal folk art and peasant culture. Like Lamming, she attributes the genesis of Caribbean nationalism and the emergence of the novel to the influence of West Indian peasants. Also in agreement with Lamming's narrative of nationalist activities, Wynter's work concludes with failure rather than with triumph. She says in an essay that begins with an epigraph from *The Pleasures of Exile*, "Their failure is important. The failure of the men and women in West Indian novels is a witness to the impossible odds against which they are pitted." She concludes this insight with a sharp

137

critique of (mis)reading clichéd, conventional "triumph[s] of the human spirit" in many West Indian novels.[2] Interestingly, Wynter believes that her novel itself marks a kind of failure because she "wasn't bold enough to have broken away from the format of the realist novel." She generously goes on to call Lamming's allegorical *Water With Berries,* on the other hand, a future "masterpiece."[3]

Wynter's generosity has not always been returned by some of the male writers. James, for instance, in the same interview where he claims to be waiting, along with Lamming, for women writers to define their "occasion for speaking," dismisses Merle Hodge's *Crick Crack, Monkey,* although he does give credit to Wynter herself and to a few African-American women writers.[4] Hodge's novel is, like Wynter's, an equally successful attempt to raise some of the issues Lamming was concerned with, but it goes on to challenge the male-centered world of *In the Castle of My Skin.* In a more terse narrative than Lamming's, Tee, the autobiographical voice in Hodge's novel, describes the travails of an alienating education amidst the overpowering fear of succumbing to "ordinaryness and . . . niggeryness." But adding to Tee's worries are the constraints of being an adolescent female and having not just her inferior class and racial status to contend with, but also her subordinate position as female. In spite of having to deal with such constraints, a woman is clearly expected to master her difficulties and smoothly coordinate the running of the household and the raising of children. She is regarded as a failure if she lacks supposedly feminine, moral attributes. Tee's abrupt transference from her lower-class milieu to the more affluent but sycophantic middle-class one is characterized by the two important female figures in her life. Says Tee:

> at times I resented Tantie bitterly for not having let Auntie Beatrice get us in the first place and bring us up properly. What Auntie Beatrice said so often was quite true: how could a woman with no sense of right and wrong take it upon herself to bring up children, God knew the reason why He hadn't given her any of her own. And I was ashamed and distressed to find myself thinking of Tantie in this way.[5]

Tee's anxieties about improper upbringing rise with her introduction to the middle-class pieties of Auntie Beatrice's world. Her own guilt at thus demeaning Tantie's labor comes from memories of a poor but

fairly happy childhood under Tantie's care, unlike the current restraints of Auntie Beatrice's constant nagging.

Mothers in Lamming's novels gain a great deal of clarity when put
in this general context of women raising children, often single-hand-
edly. G. is not entirely blind to his mother's strength or to her forceful
personality. His lengthy, affectionate description of his mother's prepa-
rations for a special dinner, while she harangues him in a parental fashion, is an eloquent tribute to her. As he watches her pack for his
impending departure to Trinidad, G. says with a return to his characteristic vagueness, "I tried to remember what she was like before I left
the village school, but nothing was clear to me. I remembered she had
grown thin after I entered the High School."[6] This observation, coming
so soon after a description of the meal she prepares for him, contains
G.'s muted recognition that his gains up the social ladder have taken
their toll on his mother, the sole breadwinner of the family. Given the
novel's emphasis on the house as a metaphorical site of identity, the
place of the mother is more central to the emergent consciousness of the
adolescent than G. implies.[7] As mothers carry on the task of providing
their children with the means to participate in the nationalist struggle,
their own hardships and contributions are often forgotten.[8] Lamming
himself owed a great deal to his mother, who was primarily responsible for raising him. But mothers in many of Lamming's novels, ranging
from G.'s mother to Myra's mother, are largely domestic figures, often
overpoweringly nurturing and protective. In *Of Age*, Ma Shephard, like
Ma in *In the Castle*, is presented as a strong, aged, observer of the
island's struggles, which she then relates to the boys. But also like Ma
in the earlier novel, she distances herself from the political movement
and relies on Christian patience and endurance to pull her through. Pa
in *In the Castle* and Shephard in *Of Age* play the more acute critics of
colonial structures.

For a reading that puts women, like Fola in *Season*, in a more
activist position, we could turn to Zee Edgell's *Beka Lamb* or Michelle
Cliff's *The Land of Look Behind*. Edgell's novel insists, through a self-conscious and critical narrator, on the importance of negotiating colonial
education. The "Befo' time" of Beka's grandmother does not reduce her
to a mythical, earth mother/goddess voice of the folk, but instead
allows her to use her age in order to read historical time.[9] The impact
she has on her granddaughter is an overtly political one. Beka struggles
to enter the privileged domain of print, but her success with the essay,

marking her entry into the articulation of her own identity, does not distract her from attending rallies in the moment of universal adult suffrage that meets with such disaster in *Of Age*. Similarly, Michelle Cliff's *The Land of Look Behind*, dedicated to Audre Lorde and explicitly acknowledging its debt to the Ghanaian writer, Ama Ata Aidoo, is a militant usurpation of the language of colonial education, embodying subversive appropriation in her phrase, "spitting into their cultural soup." Cliff displays disrespect for forms of institutional authority and refuses to remain speechless. In a striking contrast to notions of skin color in *In the Castle*, though, Cliff educates us about the complexities of possessing a light complexion. She sees skin itself as a garment open to subversion and refers to it as camouflage: "To this day camouflage terrorizes me. / The pattern of skin which makes a being invisible against its habitat. / And—yes—this camouflage exists for its protection. I am not what I seem to be." But she is also read negatively as someone who does not look black and therefore does not look Jamaican enough.[10] The inauthenticity read into her skin color is transferred to her identity, and while Cliff chooses to display defiantly the contaminated contours of her identity, the position of the light-skinned Creole does not seem as unvaryingly privileged as one might assume in the darkened world of G. and his friends. She herself argues that while light skin color was associated with the superiority of whiteness in the color politics of Jamaica, it did not really make her white. Cliff's sexuality also complicates the picture of a supposedly authentic Caribbean identity. Refusals to respect her sexual difference are a sober reminder of the uneasiness of so-called hybrid and multiple identities usually considered representative of the postmodern Caribbean.

While G. is bemused by his encounter with the High School, in *Beka Lamb*, Toycie, a bright student, is destroyed not by colonial education, but by the irresponsibility of a young man who makes her pregnant and then abandons her. As Lamming's *Water With Berries* and *Season* show with such potency, the violence of colonial displacement is heightened by the acts of violence against women. The rapes of Myra and Fola's mother in these novels alter the sympathetic portrayal of the male characters ravaged by colonial dominance. *Season*, more than any other novel by Lamming, allows a woman to emerge as a distinct subject, reminding us that women also actively participated in the nationalist struggles. They did not, however, always benefit from them when their position was quickly subsumed in the homogenizing rhetoric of national belonging. The novelist does not hesitate to critique himself and others for the selective vision of women in earlier works. He says in a speech in 1987, pointing to his own novel as an example of the blindness to women's work, *"In the Castle of My Skin* . . . [is] dominated by boys, there is no reference at all to girls. And it has taken critics a long time to notice this absence."[11] Although I believe that Lamming is generally hard to place in any kind of rigid developmental scheme, his views regarding the place of women have undergone a self-conscious shift to which he himself draws attention.[12]

Lamming provides an alternative to some of his depictions of women as violated objects in his most explicit critique of gender relations, *Natives of My Person.* Weaving domestic tensions and failed power struggles with women into the general oppressiveness of the colonial sphere, he portrays the megalomania of male colonizers as literally spreading across the globe like a plague. Although his female characters in the novel display their own blindnesses to the congealed yet threatening mass of "natives," they also serve as a warning about the terrifying potential of power unleashed without conscience. Commenting on the gaps in the knowledge of the Commandant and his other officers, who are ironically engaged in constructing knowledges about their subordinates and slaves, the Lady of the House declares to her female companions, "We are a future they must learn."[13] The Lady's specific reference to the women in the novel does not preclude the possibility of other gaps in colonial knowledge, as the final convergence of the shipwrecked women, the mutinous mariners, and the rebellious Tribes allows all of these groups to be unified momentarily in the ethical imperatives that discipline and sensitize arrogant power. Lamming seems to indicate the interconnectedness of various injustices but does not go so far as to formulate any kind of "rainbow coalition" among the groups in question.

The future to which the Lady points is expressed through deep foreboding, and the responsibility of paying attention to the resistance of those they seek to master is placed squarely on officials with power. The moral obligation invoked by the "must" in the "we are a future they must learn" implies not just the value of the instructional process, but the dire necessity of educating oneself in the perspectives outside of one's inherited privileges. The novelist is not offering a choice here, but is issuing a challenge. And in case one mistakenly underestimates the imperative behind the Lady's statement, the reader might recall the fate of the officials who ignore the necessity of such learning. Lamming's sense of the seriousness of his work is articulated through its pedagogical necessity. Postcolonial critiques such as his offer obligatory lessons on both sides of the Middle Passage.

Lamming's position in the trajectory of postcolonial writing from the Caribbean is a liminal one, standing between the gradual end of colonial rule and the cracks that began to show in nationalism soon after independence. His novels irregularly chart that trajectory from a determined protest against colonial intervention and the inheritance of a slave past to the complicated recognition of a new future in the Caribbean, still marked by a colonial legacy. While some of his works demonstrate an affinity for black nationalism, *Of Age* illustrates his regional sympathies for a Pan-Caribbean politics that make space for the diversity of cultures. Standing on the threshold of the colonial period, as his statements on Rodney's murder indicate, Lamming does not see the door shut firmly after the formal end of colonialism. He says:

> There has been little change, over the centuries, in the way the Caribbean has been perceived by metropolitan powers. It has been regarded as an imperial frontier, an island chain of fortresses which might ensure safe passage to some other destination; an experiment in European capitalism overseas; or a congenial harbor where military exercises are rehearsed to remind us and our mainland neighbors that the poor are weak, and resistance, in the name of sovereignty, is not a game they can play without the risk of being eliminated.
>
> Today, the United States argues that this Region is an absolute logistical necessity for protecting the national security interests of that country. And the peoples of the Caribbean who, through the investment of their labor and various stages of liberation from bondage, struggled to make a home of that landscape, have from time to time been forced or persuaded to share this view of the Region as an imperial frontier.[14]

Lamming's perception of the continued manufacture of the region as a gateway for metropolitan powers puts an ironic twist to Antonio Benitez-Rojo's postmodern celebration of the Caribbean as "the repeating island."[15] Benitez-Rojo's notion of repetition with a difference veers away from Lamming's more grim sense of the Caribbean as caught in the stranglehold of forces that may be different but have the same consequences. In the familiar images of tourist advertising, the carnivalesque space is precisely one more configuration of the "imperial frontier" of the Caribbean. Its laughter, gaiety, music, dance, and flexibility function as a double-edged sword, both embodying a resistance to the deprivation of colonial culture and representing exactly what is appropriated by a tourist discourse that reifies these characteristics.

Lamming offers a different perspective of the carnivalized black body in *Water With Berries*. Roger, the Indian from San Cristobal, wastes his musical talent in the indifferent metropolis of London. But in a provocative passage, Lamming indicates a larger wastefulness on the part of Roger, who has fled from San Cristobal to the apparent shelter of the English metropolis. Encountering Roger on the streets, a stranger, a black man, inquires about his profession. He explodes when he hears that Roger is a musician. He tells a startled Roger, "Give me a law and I amputate every dancin' nigger from his legs. An' singin' likewise. I against all that activity which makes niggers swap play for power." A little later, he snaps, "If 'tis musical instruments niggers need they must learn the gun. That makes a sound to some real purpose."[16] Lamming's indictment of San Cristobal's art as performed in London seems to critique his own position in the metropolis as inappropriate, given the tasks of nation building at home. The anxiety about being removed from activist politics at home as a result of exile is apparent not just in the attack on Roger's profession, but also in the long argument between Teeton and Jeremy. In an interview, Lamming himself talks about urging students at a West Indian university not to leave the islands and expresses concern for what he sees as a loss of potential in the Caribbean through migration. But in the same interview, he is not optimistic about conditions for publication at home.[17] However, as his own return to the Caribbean suggests, Lamming seems to read return as a necessary step for himself, although he undermines any romanticized notions of homecoming in his novels. Consequently, while Lamming's analysis of the condition of migrants in England shares much with the later generation of diaspora-oriented black intellectuals such as Paul Gilroy and Stuart Hall, his return to the Caribbean is indicative of a nationalistic divide between generations. While the earlier generation is more prone to be nostalgic about the "home" of the Caribbean and construct it through the idea of rootedness, however rhizomic, with some exceptions, the children of migrants who grew up in England are more likely to see the latter as their home, however unwelcoming and dysfunctional.[18] Their nostalgia, if any, for the Caribbean is necessarily different.

The stranger's challenge in *Water With Berries* is not as foreboding to Lamming's artistic production as it sounds. After *Natives*, which was published more than a decade after the publication of *Season* and which itself preceded *Water* by a year, no novels have been forthcoming so far. But Lamming is far from having retired as a public intellectual and creative writer. He continues to travel, to write, to teach, and to lecture all over the world, though he has made his base back in Barbados in an apparent commitment to the daily politics of the region. Viewing a return of the scattered diaspora of artists as a good sign, Lamming credits Eric Williams with starting "the pattern of reunions which has brought us here." Welcoming artists from all over the Caribbean as part of the same family, the novelist seems to be in no danger of giving up the pen for the gun, as we might be led to think if we took the stranger's comment too literally. Lamming says, "While the soldier may applaud stability with his gun, the creative, cultural worker forces us to question the content of that stability, to rethink, even to redefine the terms of our meaning." He goes on, "The grave is, after all, a very stable place, perhaps the most stable of places. But it would be a strange intelligence which chose the cemetery as a model kingdom of development."[19] He continues, therefore, to see cultural production as a necessary alternative to the violence of Caribbean history. The idea of the artist imagining a new future upon the cemetery of the past remains a conception central to Lamming's cultural work.

Notes

Introduction

1. Andaiye, foreword to *Conversations: George Lamming Essays, Addresses and Interviews 1953–1990*, ed. Richard Drayton and Andaiye (London: Karia Press, 1992), 8. The account of the funeral is borrowed from Andaiye. All further references are from this edition.
2. George Lamming, "On the Murder of Rodney," in *Conversations*, 184.
3. The term *Caribbean* is increasingly preferred over the more colonial title for the islands stretching from Jamaica to the Leewards and Windwards islands, Barbados, and Trinidad, as well as the mainland territories of the British Honduras and Guyana. The British-ruled, English-speaking territories, once denoted by the term *West Indies*, are now seen as part of the larger Caribbean. I also use the terms *West Indies/Indian*, however, in order to bring out the colonial implications of the period under survey.
4. Lamming, "The Occasion for Speaking," in *The Post-Colonial Studies Reader*, ed. Bill Ashcroft, Gareth Griffiths, and Helen Tiffin (London: Routledge, 1995), 12–17.
5. Lamming, "The Occasion for Speaking," in *The Pleasures of Exile* (1960; reprint, Ann Arbor: University of Michigan Press, 1992), 23–50. All further references are from this edition.
6. V. S. Naipaul, *The Middle Passage: Impressions of Five Societies—British, French and Dutch—in the West Indies and South America* (1962; reprint, New York: Vintage, 1981).
7. Lamming, "Conversation with George Lamming," interview by Daryl Cumber Dance in *New World Adams: Conversations with Contemporary West Indian Writers*, ed. Daryl Cumber Dance (Yorkshire: Peepal Tree, 1992), 135. Lamming first criticizes Hearne in *Pleasures*, 45.
8. Sidney W. Mintz, "The Caribbean Region," in *Slavery, Colonialism, and Racism*, ed. Sidney W. Mintz (New York: W. W. Norton and Co., 1974), 50, 62, 45.

9. J. M. Bernstein, *The Philosophy of the Novel: Lukács, Marxism and the Dialectics of Form* (Minneapolis: University of Minnesota Press, 1984), 27, 28 (emphasis in original), 33.

10. Lamming, introduction to *In the Castle of My Skin* (1953; reprint, Ann Arbor: University of Michigan Press, 1991), xlvi, xliv. All further references are from this edition.

11. Henry Louis Gates Jr., "Critical Fanonism," *Critical Inquiry* 17 (Spring 1991): 457–70. I have known readers of *In the Castle* who have been convinced that Lamming must have read Frantz Fanon's *The Wretched of the Earth* before writing the novel, or else they argue, when one points out that Lamming's novel was published a good ten years or so before Fanon's work, that it functions as an uncanny literary prediction of Fanon's theories. The point, of course, is not to squabble over what came first, but to note that the chicken and the egg, in this case, are closely related in their concerns. There is no one unique source of emergence, but rather, intimate associations and networks among these intellectuals. Thus, while keeping their specific contexts in mind, it should come as no surprise that various intellectuals were coming to the same conclusions about the demise of colonial rule on their own and also reading and influencing one another.

12. Gayatri Chakravorty Spivak, "The New Historicism: Political Commitment and the Postmodern Critic," in *The New Historicism*, ed. H. Aram Veeser (New York: Routledge, 1989), 283. Although the term *subaltern* has now come to be associated with the South Asian context of the Subaltern Studies Group, I extend the use of this Gramscian term to the peasant context of the West Indies, by no means suggesting that what it means in one context is identical to what it means in another.

13. Lamming refers to C. L. R. James, *The Black Jacobins: Toussaint L'Ouverture and the San Domingo Revolution*, rev. ed. (New York: Vintage, 1989). See *Pleasures*, 119.

14. Eric Hobsbawm, introduction to *The Invention of Tradition*, ed. Eric Hobsbawm and Terence Ranger (Cambridge: Cambridge University Press, 1983), 1–14.

15. Michel de Certeau, *The Writing of History*, trans. Tom Conley (New York: Columbia University Press, 1988), xxv.

16. Lamming, "Texas Dialogues," in *Conversations*, 60. Full citations for reprinted pieces, such as this interview, are provided in *Conversations*. Not all of them are completely faithful to the originals.

17. Frantz Fanon, *The Wretched of the Earth*, trans. Constance Farrington (Middlesex, England: Penguin, 1967), 28.

18. Lamming, "A Visit to Carriacou," in *Conversations*, 25.

19. Ironically, when Lamming does bring Myra/Miranda's mother to life in his novel, *Water With Berries*, she turns out to be a female counterpart to the tyrannical Prospero.

20. Paul Ricoeur, "Imagination in Dicourse and in Action," in *Rethinking Imagination: Culture and Creativity*, ed. Gillian Robinson and John Rundell (London: Routledge, 1994), 125.

21. Wilson Harris, *History, Fable and Myth in the Caribbean and Guianas* (Georgetown, Guyana: The National History and Arts Council/Ministry of Information and Culture, 1970), 8. For more extensive work on his theories of the imagination, see Wilson Harris, *The Radical Imagination: Lectures and Talks*, ed. Alan Riach and Mark Williams (Belgium: L³—Liège Language and Literature, 1992).

22. Harris, *History*, 8, 9.

23. For a reading of limbo theory applied to Caribbean modernism, see Simon Gikandi,

Writing in Limbo: Modernism and Caribbean Literature (Ithaca, N.Y.: Cornell University Press, 1992). The book also includes one of the most detailed discussions of narrative strategies in some of Lamming's novels.

24. Lamming, "A Future They Must Learn," interview with George Kent, in *Conversations*, 100.

25. Lamming comes from a Marxist position, but refutes the centrality of Marx in his awareness of class issues, which he thinks are less original in Marxism than the notion of human production of history through work. He says, "But I did not discover how class society deforms human relations from Marx. I lived it." See "A Visit to Carriacou," in *Conversations*, 26. Lamming himself, says Andaiye in the foreword to *Conversations*, was treated with suspicion by some Marxists who felt he did not sufficiently toe the party line (11).

26. Lamming, "Caribbean Literature: The Black Rock of Africa," in *Conversations*, 125.

27. Locating the modern novel in its connection to irony, Georg Lukács, quoting Goethe, contrasts the divine world with the demonic one:

It [the demonic] was not divine . . . for it seemed irrational; it was not human, for it had no reason; not devilish, for it was beneficent; not angelic, for it often allowed room for malice. It resembled the accidental, for it was without consequence; it looked like providence, for it hinted at hidden connections.

See Lukács, *The Theory of the Novel: A Historico-Philosophical Essay on the Forms of Great Epic Literature*, trans. Anna Bostock (Cambridge, Mass.: MIT Press, 1971), 87.

28. Derek Walcott, *The Antilles: Fragments of Epic Memory*. The Nobel Lecture (New York: Farrar, Straus and Giroux, 1992).

29. Derek Walcott, "What the Twilight Says: An Overture," in *Dream on Monkey Mountain and Other Plays* (New York: Farrar, Straus and Giroux, 1970), 8.

30. Derek Walcott, "The Muse of History," in *Is Massa Day Dead? Black Moods in the Caribbean*, ed. Orde Coombes (New York: Anchor/Doubleday, 1974), 1.

31. Richard Drayton, introduction to *Conversations*, 20.

32. Richard Hakluyt, *The Principal Navigations, Voyages, Traffiques, and Discoveries of the English Nation*, 12 vols. (Glasgow: MacLehose, 1903–1905).

33. J. Michael Dash, introduction to *Caribbean Discourse: Selected Essays* by Edouard Glissant, trans. J. Michael Dash (Charlottesville: University Press of Virginia, 1989), xiii.

34. Lamming, "Conversation with George Lamming," in *New World Adams*, 138.

35. Lamming, "On the Murder of Rodney," in *Conversations*, 184.

36. Antonio Gramsci, *Selections from the Prison Notebooks*, trans. Quintin Hoare and Geoffrey Nowell Smith (New York: International Publishers, 1971), 9.

37. Lamming, "Western Education and the Caribbean Intellectual." Unpublished lecture. I am grateful to George Lamming for giving me a copy of this lecture.

38. Sandra Pouchet Paquet, foreword to *In the Castle*, xii.

39. Similarly, Lamming believes that the allegory in *Natives* applies to the contemporary corruption and power struggles of Caribbean leaders. See "A Future," in *Conversations*, 86–87.

40. I agree with Reinhard W. Sander, who claims, in his excellent study of the thirties, that it was a turbulent and creative period, both politically and in terms of literary

output. Nevertheless, Lamming does have a point when he argues that writers were largely alienated from public attention. See Reinhard Sander, *The Trinidad Awakening: West Indian Literature of the Nineteen-Thirties* (New York: Greenwood Press, 1988).

41. Lamming is even more blunt when it comes to discussing the death of Roger Mais, from Jamaica, who died of cancer while in exile: "They murdered Roger Mais and they know it" (*Pleasures,* 41). Drawing links between Mittelholzer, himself, and other writers across the Caribbean, Lamming says of his audience:

> On the one hand a mass of people who were either illiterate, or if not had no con-
> nection whatever to literature since they were too poor or too tired to read; and on
> the other hand a colonial middle-class educated, it seemed, for the specific purpose
> of sneering at anything which grew or was made on native soil (40).

42. Lamming, "C. L. R. James, Evangelist," in *Conversations,* 200.
43. Lamming, interview by the author, tape recording, Miami, Florida, July 6, 1992.
44. James, "Interview with C. L. R. James," by Ian Munro and Reinhard Sander in *Kas-Kas: Interviews with Three Caribbean Writers in Texas: George Lamming, C. L. R. James, Wilson Harris* (Austin, Tex.: African and Afro-American Research Institute, 1972), 24.
45. Edward W. Said, *Culture and Imperialism* (New York: Alfred A. Knopf, 1993), 209, 214, 212.
46. Andaiye, foreword to *Conversations,* 15.
47. I cannot engage here in the complex debate about the postcolonial and the postmodern. Briefly, I would agree with Kumkum Sangari that the two terms cannot be conflated and that they operate within historically specific contexts. Nevertheless, in a broadly general way, the constant disruption in narrative strategies is something that they share in common. See Kumkum Sangari, "The Politics of the Possible," *Cultural Critique* 7 (Fall 1987): 157–86.
48. Lamming, *Of Age and Innocence* (1958; reprint, New York: Allison and Busby, 1970), 13.
49. Ngũgĩ wa Thiong'o, *Decolonising the Mind: The Politics of Language in African Literature* (London: James Currey, 1986).
50. Dipesh Chakrabarty, "Postcoloniality and the Artifice of History: Who Speaks for 'Indian' Pasts?," *Representations* 37 (Winter 1992): 18–19.
51. Gordon Rohlehr makes one of the first critiques of Lamming's declaration that the West Indian novel "restores" the peasants to history. Arguing that there is no general peasant sensibility that one can capture, he suggests that Lamming might more appropriately talk about reflecting rather than restoring the peasants to their "original status." See Rohlehr, "The Folk in Caribbean Literature," in *Critical Perspectives on Sam Selvon,* ed. Susheila Nasta (Washington, D.C.: Three Continents Press, 1988), 32. Reprinted from *Tapia* (17 Dec. 1972): 7–8, 13–14.
52. I use the phrase "calling up some spirits" metaphorically in this case, exploiting Lamming's insistence on the ritual as a symbolic means of bringing back absent and/or unheard voices. I think it is a useful metaphor for the same reason, but I do not mean to imply that it has more than an imaginative connection to the practice of Vodoun, which is a material practice with a specificity of its own. Also, my critique of Lam-

ming here is not a question of his being fair to women (or peasants) or accurately representing "real" life but uses his own critical sense of the politics of representation in colonial culture and extends it to so-called native women.

53. Sylvia Wynter, Afterword, "Beyond Miranda's Meanings: Un/silencing the 'Demonic Ground' of Caliban's 'Woman,'" in *Out of the Kumbla: Caribbean Women and Literature,* ed. Carole Boyce Davies and Elaine Savory Fido (Trenton, N.J.: Africa World Press, 1990), 360.

Chapter 1

1. George Lamming, "The Occasion for Speaking," in *The Pleasures of Exile* (1960; reprint, Ann Arbor: University of Michigan Press, 1992), 36–37.

2. Richard Helgerson, "Camoes, Hakluyt, and the Voyages of Two Nations," in *Colonialism and Culture,* ed. Nicholas B. Dirks (Ann Arbor: University of Michigan Press, 1992), 27.

3. Peter Hulme, *Colonial Encounters: Europe and the Native Caribbean, 1492–1797* (1986; reprint, London: Routledge, 1992), 3.

4. Mary Louise Pratt, *Imperial Eyes: Travel Writing and Transculturation* (London: Routledge, 1992), 29. Pratt defines circumnavigation as a double deed that consisted of sailing around the world and writing an account of it. This, along with activities like mapping, contributed to the construction of the European planetary subject.

5. Benedict Anderson, *Imagined Communities: Reflections on the Origin and Spread of Nationalism,* rev. ed. (London: Verso, 1991), 37.

6. Pratt, *Imperial Eyes,* 29–30. Pratt classifies the "global subject" of this expansionist period as "European, male, secular, and lettered." Although *Natives* necessarily provides variations, the construction of the global subject in the Commandant is similar to Pratt's categorization.

7. Karl Marx, *Capital: A Critique of Political Economy,* Vol.1, trans. Ben Fowkes (New York: Vintage, 1976), 911, 915.

8. Stephen Slemon, "Monuments of Empire: Allegory/Counter-Discourse/Post-colonial Writing," *Kunapipi* 9, no. 3 (1987), 11.

9. Fredric Jameson, "Third-World Literature in the Era of Multinational Capitalism," *Social Text* 15 (1986), 69. Aijaz Ahmad's critique, "Jameson's Rhetoric of Otherness and the 'National Allegory,'" was published in a subsequent issue of *Social Text* (Fall 1987), with a brief response by Jameson.

10. Slemon, "Monuments," 13.

11. George Lamming, *Natives of My Person* (1972; reprint, Ann Arbor: University of Michigan Press, 1992), 4. All references are from this edition.

12. I am summarizing Gay Clifford in *The Transformations of Allegory* (London: Routledge and Kegan Paul, 1974), 11. She essentially argues against the perception of allegory as static and conservative. Also see, on adventure narratives, Martin Green, *Dreams of Adventure, Deeds of Empire* (New York: Basic Books, 1979).

13. Anderson, *Imagined Communities,* 86.

14. "Quite often, a Hakluyt, or any of those men reporting those voyages, never realized how ironic that exercise would be to a later reader," says Lamming in an interview by

George Kent. "A Future They Must Learn," in *Conversations: George Lamming Essays, Addresses and Interviews, 1953–1990,* ed. Richard Drayton and Andaiye (London: Karia Press, 1992), 95.

15. Richard Ligon, *A True and Exact History of Barbados* (London: Humphrey Moseley, 1657).

16. Hulme, *Colonial Encounters,* 57. He uses this anthropological term to suggest that nonextant, nonliterate societies have not left many narratives that describe their way of life from their point of view. The question, "Who are you?" cannot, therefore, be answered in the first-person, thus making self-ascription unavailable.

17. From Eric Williams, ed., *Documents of West Indian History, 1492–1655, Vol. 1* (Trinidad: PNM Publishing Co., 1963), 254.

18. John Poyer, *The History of Barbados from the First Discovery of the Island in the Year 1605 till the Accession of Lord Seaforth 1801* (1808; reprint, London: Frank Cass, 1971), 12. Most of the details of the island's early history I borrow from Poyer. While the distant power of the sovereign is evident in the various bequests of the island, the competition for possession of the island reveals the early signs of dispute with "Mother England" and within the incipient colony itself. For another account of the establishment of plantocracy in Barbados and its initial relationship to the Stuart dynasty, see Gary A. Puckrein, *Little England: Plantation Society and Anglo-Barbadian Politics, 1627–1700* (New York: New York University Press, 1984).

19. Michel de Certeau, *Heterologies: Discourse on the Other,* trans. Brian Massumi (Minneapolis: University of Minnesota Press, 1986), 69.

20. bell hooks, quoting herself in *Yearning: Race, Gender, and Cultural Politics* (Boston: South End, 1990), 149.

21. Lamming, "A Future," 92, 95.

22. Richard Hakluyt, *The Principal Navigations, Voyages, Traffiques, and Discoveries of the English Nation,* 12 vols. (Glasgow: MacLehose, 1903–1905).

23. Irwin R. Blacker, ed., *The Portable Hakluyt's Voyages* (New York: Viking, 1965), 14.

24. Ibid., 19–20.

25. Ibid., 189.

26. Ibid., 132.

27. Daniel P. Mannix, in collaboration with Malcolm Cowley, *Black Cargoes: A History of the Atlantic Slave Trade, 1518–1865* (New York: Viking, 1962), 127.

28. Lamming, "A Future," 88.

29. Lamming, *The Pleasures of Exile* (1960; reprint, Ann Arbor: University of Michigan Press, 1992), 114.

30. Blacker, *Portable Voyages,* 417.

31. Cowley, *Black Cargoes,* x.

32. Blacker, *Portable Voyages,* 46.

33. V. T. Harlow, *A History of Barbados, 1625–1685* (Oxford: Clarendon Press, 1926), 295.

34. Sandra Pouchet Paquet points out that Tate de Lysle has been obviously marked by "Tate and Lyle, the British sugar company founded in 1921, with the merger of two nineteenth-century British sugar firms founded by Henry Tate and Bram Lyle." See Sandra Pouchet Paquet, *The Novels of George Lamming* (London: Heinemann, 1982), 115, n. 14.

35. For details, see Buchanan Sharp, *In Contempt of All Authority: Rural Artisans and Riot in the West of England, 1586–1660* (Berkeley: University of California Press, 1980).

36. Aime Cesaire, *Discourse on Colonialism*, trans. Joan Pinkham (New York: Monthly Review Press, 1972), 20. Emphasis in original.

37. Lamming, "A Future," 86.

38. I am grateful to Paul Kintzele for tracking down the various references to faulty vision in the novel.

39. Joel Fineman, "The Structure of Allegorical Desire," in *Allegory and Representation*, ed. Stephen J. Greenblatt (Baltimore: Johns Hopkins University Press, 1981), 35.

40. Cowley, *Black Cargoes*, ix.

Chapter 2

1. C. L. R. James, preface to *Beyond a Boundary* (1963; reprint, Durham, N.C.: Duke University Press, 1993).

2. While Lamming is aware of the material and other privileges of migration to the metropolis, he chooses to focus on the illusion of the migratory dream in the novels under discussion. This is not to deny the success stories of migration to England or elsewhere, although Lamming does seem skeptical of too simple a narrative of triumph.

3. Rob Nixon, "Caribbean and African Appropriations of *The Tempest*," *Critical Inquiry* 13 (Spring 1987): 578.

4. George Lamming, *The Pleasures of Exile* (1960; reprint, Ann Arbor: University of Michigan Press, 1992), 13.

5. Ibid., 41, emphasis in original.

6. V. S. Naipaul, *The Middle Passage: Impressions of Five Societies—British, French and Dutch—in the West Indies and South America* (1962; reprint, New York: Vintage, 1981), 224.

7. Lamming, *The Emigrants* (1954; reprint, Ann Arbor: University of Michigan Press, 1994), 5. All further references are from this edition.

8. William Shakespeare, *The Tempest* 1.2. ll. 331–39. From *The Riverside Shakespeare* (Boston: Houghton Mifflin, 1974).

9. Frantz Fanon, *The Wretched of the Earth*, trans. Constance Farrington (Middlesex: Penguin, 1967), 30.

10. Ambalavaner Sivanandan, *A Different Hunger: Writings on Black Resistance* (London: Pluto, 1982), 64–65.

11. Caryl Phillips, *The Final Passage* (New York: Penguin, 1985).

12. T. S. Eliot, "Four Quartets," in *The Complete Poems and Plays, 1909–1950* (San Diego: Harcourt Brace Jovanovich, 1952), 144–45.

13. Ernest Renan, "What Is a Nation?," trans. Martin Thom, in *Nation and Narration*, ed. Homi K. Bhabha (London: Routledge, 1990), 19.

14. Lamming, *Water With Berries* (1971; reprint, London: Longman Caribbean, 1973), 70. All further references are from this edition.

15. Merle Hodge, *Crick Crack, Monkey* (London: Heinemann, 1970), 110–11.

16. In India, for instance, announcements of departures (including business trips) to Eng-

land or to the United States were made in newspapers, complete with congratulations, bon voyages, and a photograph of the lucky traveler. A quick survey of matrimonial ads in Indian newspapers will illustrate the cultural and cash value of being "settled abroad," especially with a green card.

17. Kobena Mercer, *Welcome to the Jungle: New Positions in Black Cultural Studies* (New York: Routledge, 1994), 7, emphasis in original.

18. Louise Bennett, *Selected Poems,* ed. Mervyn Morris (Kingston, Jamaica: Sangster's Book Stores, 1982), 108.

19. As I write this section, the recent shift in Congressional representation in the United States (1994) has been made amidst an apparent crisis of national identity. Proposition 187 in California and other proposals targeting immigrants, legal and illegal, rehearse much of the rhetoric that I discuss here.

20. John Solomos et al., introduction to *The Empire Strikes Back: Race and Racism in Seventies Britain* (1982; reprint, London: Hutchinson and the Centre for Contemporary Cultural Studies in Birmingham, 1983), 14.

21. Errol Lawrence, "Just Plain Common Sense: The 'Roots' of Racism," in *The Empire Strikes Back: Race and Racism in Seventies Britain,* 87.

22. Lamming, in an interview with George Kent, "A Future They Must Learn," in *Conversations: George Lamming Essays Addresses and Interviews, 1953–1990,* ed. Richard Drayton and Andaiye (London: Karia Press, 1992), 100. See also "Conversation with George Lamming," in *New World Adams: Conversations with Contemporary West Indian Writers,* ed. Daryl Cumber Dance (Yorkshire: Peepal Press, 1992), 138.

23. Lamming, "A Future," 100.

24. Frantz Fanon, *Black Skin, White Masks,* trans. Charles Lam Markmann (New York: Grove Weidenfeld, 1967), 63.

25. Lamming, "A Future," 100.

26. Edward Said, *Culture and Imperialism* (New York: Alfred A. Knopf, 1993), 213.

27. Ibid., 211.

28. Errol Francis, "Psychiatric Racism and Social Police: Black People and the Psychiatric Services," in *Inside Babylon: The Caribbean Diaspora in Britain,* ed. Winston James and Clive Harris (London: Verso, 1993), 179–205.

29. Lamming, introduction to *In the Castle of My Skin* (1953; reprint, Ann Arbor: University of Michigan Press, 1991), xxxviii.

30. Lamming, "A Future," 98.

31. Lamming, *Pleasures,* 214.

32. Through an oversight, the American and British versions of the novel have different endings. The American version (Holt, Rinehart and Winston, 1972) ends with the chapter dealing with Teeton's escape. The British edition (Longman, 1971, 1973) contains one additional chapter, a single page long, that says in four separate one-line paragraphs that the publican of Mona dies (as a result, one assumes, of burns endured in the fire set by Roger) soon after the Old Dowager's remains are found; that Derek "alone" is not charged with murder; that the Secret Gathering maintains Teeton's innocence; and that they were all waiting for the trials to begin. See Sandra Pouchet Paquet, *The Novels of George Lamming* (London: Heinemann, 1982), 98, n. 17.

Chapter 3

1. Frantz Fanon, *The Wretched of the Earth,* trans. Constance Farrington (Middlesex: Penguin, 1967), 40.

2. Edward Baugh, "The West Indian Writer and His Quarrel with History," *Tapia* 7, no. 9 (Feb. 1977): 6.

3. See Thomas Carlyle's essay, "Occasional Discourse on the Negro Question," published anonymously in *Frazer's Magazine* in December 1849. Reprinted in *Caribbean Review* 4, nos. 1–2 (April–June 1972): 19–23; Anthony Trollope's *The West Indies and the Spanish Main* (New York: Harper and Brothers, 1860); James Anthony Froude's *The English in the West Indies, or the Bow of Ulysses* (London: Longmans, Green, and Co., 1888).

4. George Lamming, introduction to *In the Castle of My Skin* (1953; reprint, Ann Arbor: University of Michigan Press, 1991), xxxvii. All further references are from this edition.

5. James Baldwin, quoted from *Notes of a Native Son,* in *The Pleasures of Exile* (1960; reprint, Ann Arbor: University of Michigan Press, 1992), 31.

6. Gordon K. Lewis, *The Growth of the Modern West Indies* (New York: Monthly Review Press, 1968), 70.

7. Carolyn T. Brown, "The Myth of the Fall and the Dawning of Consciousness in George Lamming's *In the Castle of My Skin,*" *World Literature Today* 57, no. 1 (Winter 1983), 41.

8. Fanon, *The Wretched,* 30.

9. Hilary Beckles, *A History of Barbados: From Amerindian Settlement to Nation-State* (Cambridge: Cambridge University Press, 1990), 114.

10. Eric Williams, *From Columbus to Castro: The History of the Caribbean, 1492–1969* (1970; reprint, New York: Vintage, 1984), 447, 450.

11. Nathaniel Weekes, "Barbados," in *The Penguin Book of Caribbean Verse in English,* ed. Paula Burnett (Middlesex: Penguin, 1986), 102–3.

12. Lamming, *Pleasures,* 79, 81.

13. Eugene D. Genovese, *Roll, Jordan, Roll: The World the Slaves Made* (1972; reprint, New York: Vintage, 1976), 4.

14. Lamming, introduction to *In the Castle,* xxxviii.

15. Ibid., xlvi.

16. G. W. F. Hegel, *Lectures on the Philosophy of History,* trans. J. Sibree (New York: Henry G. Bohn, 1857), 103. See also his comments on African religions, reduced to naive fetishism and frenzy in the same section (98–102).

17. Louis Althusser, "Ideology and Ideological State Apparatuses (Notes Towards an Investigation)," in *Lenin and Philosophy and Other Essays,* trans. Ben Brewster (New York: Monthly Review Press, 1971), 127–86.

18. Antonio Gramsci, *Selections from the Prison Notebooks,* trans. Quintin Hoare and Geoffrey Nowell Smith (New York: International Publishers, 1971), 39.

19. Lamming, *Pleasures,* 42, emphasis in original.

20. C. L. R. James, *Beyond a Boundary* (1963; reprint, Durham, N.C.: Duke University Press, 1993), 29–30, emphasis in original.

21. Hazel V. Carby, "Proletarian or Revolutionary Literature: C. L. R. James and the Politics of the Trinidadian Renaissance," *South Atlantic Quarterly* 87, no. 1 (Winter 1988): 39–52.

22. Lamming, *Pleasures,* 39.

23. Lamming, interview with Robert E. Lee, "Caribbean Politics from the 1930s to the 1970s," in *Conversations: George Lamming Essays, Addresses and Interviews, 1953–1990,* ed. Richard Drayton and Andaiye (London: Karia Press, 1992), 266.

24. Beckles, *A History of Barbados,* 165.

25. W. A. Lewis, *Labour in the West Indies: The Birth of a Worker's Movement* (London: Fabian Society, 1939), 15–16.

26. Fanon, *The Wretched,* 27

27. Ibid., 56.

28. Lamming, introduction to *In the Castle,* xxxvi.

29. Oddly enough, one of the first significant novels to emerge on the issue of modern colonial education for women in the Caribbean, Merle Hodge's *Crick Crack, Monkey,* was dismissed by C. L. R. James in an interview with Daryl Cumber Dance in *New World Adams: Conversations with Contemporary West Indian Writers* (Yorkshire, England: Peepal Tree Books, 1992), 118.

30. Lamming, introduction to *In the Castle,* xxxix, xl.

31. Lewis, *The Growth of the Modern West Indies,* 242.

32. Lamming, "Caribbean Politics," 267.

33. Ibid., 267.

34. Fanon, *The Wretched,* 96.

35. Lamming, *Pleasures,* 228.

Chapter 4

1. George Lamming, *Of Age and Innocence* (1958; reprint, London: Allison and Busby, 1981), 54. All further references are from this edition.

2. Lamming, *The Pleasures of Exile* (1960; reprint, Ann Arbor: University of Michigan Press, 1992), 12.

3. Derek Walcott, quoted by Edward Baugh in "The West Indian Writer and His Quarrel with History," *Tapia* 7, no. 8 (Feb. 1977): 6.

4. Roberto Fernández Retamar, "Caliban: Notes Towards a Discussion of Culture in Our America," trans. Lynn Garafola et al., *The Massachussets Review* 15, nos. 1–2 (Winter–Spring 1974): 33.

5. Homi Bhabha, "Introduction: Narrating the Nation," in *Nation and Narration,* ed. Homi Bhabha (London: Routledge, 1990), 1, 2, emphasis in original.

6. Although both Benedict Anderson and Eric Hobsbawm examine invention and imagination predominantly from the dominant cultural perspective, neither of them foreclose their potential for resistance and subversion among subordinate populations. See Anderson, *Imagined Communities: Reflections on the Origin and Spread of Nationalism,* rev. ed. (London: Verso, 1991) and Hobsbawm and Terence Ranger, ed., *The Invention of Tradition* (1983; reprint, Cambridge: Cambridge University Press, 1992).

7. Lamming, *Season of Adventure* (1960; reprint, London: Allison and Busby, 1979), 16. All further references are from this edition.

8. Wilson Harris, *History, Fable and Myth in the Caribbean and Guianas* (Georgetown, Guyana: The National History and Arts Council/Ministry of Information and Culture, 1970), 10.

9. Raymond Williams, *Marxism and Literature* (Oxford: Oxford University Press, 1977), 122–23.

10. Frantz Fanon, *The Wretched of the Earth,* trans. Constance Farrington (Middlesex: Penguin, 1967), 183.

11. Paul Gilroy, *The Black Atlantic: Modernity and Double Consciousness* (Cambridge, Mass.: Harvard University Press, 1993), 199. Gilroy, unlike Fanon, however, articulates the nation from within a postmodern, postindustrial space in which geographical borders are not absolute. I owe a great deal to his theories of the revolutionary potential of music and its connection to slavery.

12. Kamau Brathwaite, "The African Presence in Caribbean Literature," in *Roots* (Ann Arbor: University of Michigan Press, 1993), 190–91.

13. V. S. Naipaul, *The Middle Passage: Impressions of Five Societies—British, French and Dutch—in the West Indies and South America* (1962; reprint, New York: Vintage, 1981), 41.

14. Lamming, *Pleasures,* 32–33.

15. Fanon, *The Wretched,* 180, 175.

16. Derek Walcott, "What the Twilight Says: An Overture," in *Dream on Monkey Mountain and Other Plays* (New York: Farrar, Strauss and Giroux, 1970), 8.

17. Lamming, "Caribbean Literature: The Black Rock of Africa" in *Conversations: George Lamming Essays, Addresses and Interviews, 1953–1990,* ed. Richard Drayton and Andaiye (London: Karia Press, 1992), 125.

18. Lamming, *Pleasures,* 9.

19. Fanon, *The Wretched,* 30, 43. Emphasis added.

20. Ibid., 45.

21. See, for instance, Selwyn R. Cudjoe's *Resistance and Caribbean Literature* (Athens: Ohio University Press, 1980); Michel Laguerre's *Voodoo and Politics in Haiti* (New York: St. Martin's Press, 1989); and Patrick Taylor's *The Narrative of Liberation: Perspectives on Afro-Caribbean Literature, Popular Culture, and Politics* (Ithaca, N.Y.: Cornell University Press, 1989).

22. C. L. R. James, *The Black Jacobins: Toussaint L'Ouverture and the San Domingo Revolution,* rev. ed. (New York: Vintage, 1989), 86.

23. Lamming, *Pleasures,* 9.

24. Ibid., 12.

25. Brathwaite, *Roots,* 255. See also Paule Marshall, *The Chosen Place, The Timeless People* (1969; reprint, New York: Vintage, 1984), 106.

26. Joan Dayan, "Vodoun, or the Voice of the Gods," *Raritan* 10, no. 3 (Winter 1991): 36, 40.

27. The film *Angel Heart* (dir. Alan Parker, MCA, 1987) is one such example.

28. Michael T. Taussig, *The Devil and Commodity Fetishism in South America* (Chapel Hill: University of North Carolina Press, 1980), 31.

29. Lamming, *Pleasures*, 162.

30. Lamming, "The Makers of History," in *Conversations*, 292.

31. See "A Monster, A Child, A Slave," and "Caliban Orders History," in *Pleasures*, 95–150.

32. Kamau Brathwaite, introduction to *Life in a Haitian Valley* by Melville Herskovits (New York: Anchor Doubleday, 1971), xii–xiii.

33. Vodoun, like many other ideologies of popular resistance, has also been co-opted by the ruling elite. During the rule of "Papa Doc" (Francois Duvalier) and "Baby Doc" (Jean Claude Duvalier), in contrast to the repression that Lamming describes in the opening lines of *Pleasures*, Vodoun was used as a tool of the Haitian state.

34. Lamming, *Pleasures*, 10.

35. Ibid.

36. James C. Scott, *Domination and the Arts of Resistance: Hidden Transcripts* (New Haven, Conn.: Yale University Press, 1990).

37. Lamming, *Pleasures*, 121.

38. Dayan, "Vodoun," 39.

39. James, *The Black Jacobins*, 108.

40. Antonio Gramsci, *Selections From the Prison Notebooks*, trans. Quintin Hoare and Geoffrey Nowell Smith (New York: International Publishers, 1971), 10, 34.

41. Gramsci, "National-Popular Literature, The Popular Novel, and Observations on Folklore," in *Communication and Class Struggle*, Vol. 2, ed. Armand Mattelart and Seth Siegelaub (New York: International General, 1983), 75.

42. Sandra Pouchet Paquet notes the modular character of the name of what she calls a "wooden" character. Kofi James-Williams Baako, she says, combines the names of C. L. R. James and Eric Williams, both Trinidadian intellectual leaders, and Kofi Baako, the Ghanaian nationalist. In Paquet, *The Novels of George Lamming* (London: Heinemann, 1982), 80.

43. Baako's politicization of folk culture and its influence on the educated intellectual can also be seen in Fanon's essay, "On National Culture," in *The Wretched of the Earth*, 166–99, and in Ngũgĩ wa Thiong'o's account of the Kamĩrĩĩthũ experiment in *Decolonising the Mind: The Politics of Language in African Literature* (London: James Currey, 1986), 34–62.

44. Lamming, *Pleasures*, 47.

45. Lamming, *In the Castle of My Skin* (1953; reprint, Ann Arbor: University of Michigan Press, 1991), 213.

46. Anderson, *Imagined Communites*, 24.

47. Ibid., 23.

48. Alice Walker, "Looking for Zora," in *In Search of Our Mother's Gardens* (San Diego: Harcourt Brace Jovanovich, 1983), 93–116.

49. Henry Louis Gates Jr., afterword to *Tell My Horse: Voodoo and Life in Haiti and Jamaica* by Zora Neale Hurston (1938; reprint, New York: Harper and Row, 1990), 298.

50. Cudjoe, *Resistance*, 185.

51. Lamming, *Pleasures*, 11.

Conclusion

1. C. L. R. James, interview with Daryl Cumber Dance, "Conversation with C. L. R. James," in *New World Adams: Conversations with Contemporary West Indian Writers* (Yorkshire: Peepal Tree, 1992), 118. Emphasis in original.

2. Sylvia Wynter, "We must Learn to Sit Down Together and Talk about a Little Culture: Reflections on West Indian Writing and Criticism," *Jamaica Journal* 2 (December 1968): 31, 32. See also, Wynter, *The Hills of Hebron* (Essex, England: Longman, 1966).

3. Sylvia Wynter, interview with Daryl Cumber Dance, "Conversation with Sylvia Wynter," in *New World Adams*, 282.

4. James, "Conversation with C. L. R. James," 118.

5. Merle Hodge, *Crick Crack, Monkey* (1970; reprint, London: Heinemann, 1981), 97.

6. George Lamming, *In the Castle of My Skin* (1953; reprint, Ann Arbor: University of Michigan Press, 1991), 277.

7. For more detailed attention to the mother figure in Caribbean literature, see Carole Boyce Davies's discussion of the mother-daughter relationship and the mother's connection to the house in "Writing Home: Gender and Heritage in the Works of Afro-Caribbean/American Women Writers," in *Out of the Kumbla: Caribbean Women and Literature*, ed. Carole Boyce Davies and Elaine Savory Fido (Trenton, N.J.: Africa World Press, 1990), 59–73. See also, *Motherlands: Black Women's Writing from Africa, the Caribbean, and South Asia*, ed. Susheila Nasta (New Brunswick, N.J.: Rutgers University Press, 1991).

8. Faith Smith, in an excellent critique of C. L. R. James's intellectual influences, highlights the role his mother had played in shaping his thought, a role that was given little attention in James's general lack of attention to gender politics. See Smith, "Coming Home to the Real Thing: Gender and Intellectual Life in the Anglophone Caribbean," *South Atlantic Quarterly* 93, no. 4 (Fall 1994): 895–923.

9. Zee Edgell, *Beka Lamb* (London: Heinemann, 1982), 1.

10. Michelle Cliff, *The Land of Look Behind* (Ithaca, N.Y.: Firebrand Books, 1985), 14, 19, 70.

11. Lamming, quoted in the foreword by Andaiye in *Conversations: George Lamming Essays, Addresses and Interviews 1953–1990*, ed. Richard Drayton and Andaiye (London: Karia Press, 1992), 13.

12. In my interview with Lamming, he told me that women had forced the writers to change their discourse and recommended *Out of the Kumbla* for readings of women writers in the Caribbean. Interview by the author, tape recording, Miami, Florida, July 6, 1992.

13. Lamming, *Natives of My Person* (1972; reprint, Ann Arbor: University of Michigan Press, 1992), 345.

14. Lamming, "Inheritance and Situation: The View from 1986," in *Conversations*, 293.

15. Antonio Benitez-Rojo, *The Repeating Island: The Caribbean and the Postmodern Perspective* (Durham, N.C.: Duke University Press, 1992). The main title plays upon all of Benitez-Rojo's theoretical influences: the poststructuralist repetition with a difference, the postmodernist sense of playful flux, and the observable order of chaos theory.

16. Lamming, *Water With Berries* (1971; reprint, London: Longman Caribbean, 1973), 69.
17. Lamming, "Texas Dialogues," in *Conversations,* 74, 73.
18. For an account of generational differences among black populations in Britain in an outstanding collection of essays on the Black British, see Winston James, "Migration, Racism and Identity Formation: The Caribbean Experience in Britain," in *Inside Babylon: The Caribbean Diaspora in Britain,* ed. Winston James and Clive Harris (London: Verso, 1993), 231–87.
19. Lamming, "Builders of our Caribbean House," in *Conversations,* 159, 161.

Selected Bibliography

Ahmad, Aijaz. *In Theory: Classes, Nations, Literatures.* London: Verso, 1992.

Althusser, Louis. "Ideology and Ideological State Apparatuses (Notes Towards an Investigation)." In *Lenin and Philosophy and Other Essays,* trans, Ben Brewster, 127–86. New York: Monthly Review Press, 1971.

Anderson, Benedict. *Imagined Communties: Reflections on the Origin and Spread of Nationalism.* 1983. Rev. ed., London: Verso, 1991.

Ashcroft, Bill, Gareth Griffiths, and Helen Tiffin, ed. *The Post-colonial Studies Reader.* London: Routledge, 1995.

Bakhtin, M. M. *The Dialogic Imagination: Four Essays.* Ed. Michael Holquist, trans. Caryl Emerson and Michael Holquist. Austin, Tex.: University of Texas Press, 1981.

Barker, Francis, and Peter Hulme. "Nymphs and Reapers Heavily Vanish: The Discursive Con-Texts of *The Tempest.*" In *Alternative Shakespeares,* ed. John Drakakis, 191–205. London: Methuen, 1985.

Barker, Francis, et al., ed. *Europe and its Others.* Vol. 2. Colchester, England: University of Essex, 1985.

Baugh, Edward. "Cuckoo and Culture: *In the Castle of My Skin.*" *Ariel* 8, no. 3 (1977): 23–33.

———. "The West Indian Writer and His Quarrel with History." *Tapia* 7, nos. 8, 9 (1977).

Beckles, Hilary. *A History of Barbados: From Amerindian Settlement to Nation-State.* Cambridge, England: Cambridge University Press, 1990.

Benítez-Rojo, Antonio. *The Repeating Island: The Caribbean and the Postmodern Perspective.* Trans. James Maraniss. Durham, N.C.: Duke University Press, 1992.

Benjamin, Walter. *Illuminations.* Ed. Hannah Arendt, trans. Harry Zohn. New York: Schocken, 1968.

Bennett, Louise. *Selected Poems.* Ed. Mervyn Morris. 1982. Reprint, Kingston, Jamaica: Sangster's Book Stores, 1991.

Bernstein, J. M. *The Philosophy of the Novel: Lukacs, Marxism and the Dialectics of Form.* Minneapolis: University of Minnesota Press, 1984.

Bhabha, Homi K., ed. *Nation and Narration.* London: Routledge, 1990.

Blacker, Irwin R., ed. *The Portable Hakluyt's Voyages.* New York: Viking, 1965.

Brathwaite, Kamau. "Caliban." In *Islands,* 34–38. London: Oxford University Press, 1969.

———. *Roots.* Ann Arbor: University of Michigan Press, 1993.

Brown, Carolyn T. "The Myth of the Fall and the Dawning of Consciousness in George Lamming's *In the Castle of My Skin.*" *World Literature Today* 57, no. 1 (Winter 1983): 38–43.

Cabral, Amilcar. *Unity and Struggle: Speeches and Writings.* Trans. Michael Wolfers. London: Heinemann, 1980.

Carby, Hazel. "Proletarian or Revolutionary Literature: C. L. R. James and the Politics of the Trinidadian Renaissance." *South Atlantic Quarterly* 87, no. 1 (Winter 1988): 39–52.

Carlyle, Thomas. "Occasional Discourse on the Negro Question." 1849. Reprint, *Caribbean Review* 4, nos. 1–2 (April–June 1972): 19–23.

Cartey, Wilfred. "Lamming and the Search for Freedom." *New World Quarterly: Barbados Independence Issue* 3, nos. 1–2 (1967–68): 121–28.

Césaire, Aimé. *Discourse on Colonialism.* Trans. Joan Pinkham. New York: Monthly Review Press, 1972.

Chakrabarty, Dipesh. "Postcoloniality and the Artifice of History: Who Speaks for 'Indian' Pasts?" *Representations* 37 (Winter 1992): 1–26.

Chatterjee, Partha. *Nationalist Thought and the Colonial World: A Derivative Discourse.* Minneapolis: University of Minnesota Press, 1986.

Cliff, Michelle. *The Land of Look Behind.* Ithaca, N.Y.: Firebrand Books, 1985.

Clifford, Gay. *The Transformations of Allegory.* London: Routledge and Kegan Paul, 1974.

Cudjoe, Selwyn R. *Resistance and Caribbean Literature.* Athens: Ohio University Press, 1980.

———., ed. *Caribbean Women Writers: Essays from the First International Conference.* Wellesley, Mass.: Calaloux Publications, 1990.

Dance, Daryl Cumber, ed. *New World Adams: Conversations with Contemporary West Indian Writers,* 1984. Reprint, Yorkshire: Peepal Tree, 1992.

Dash, Michael J. "In Search of the Lost Body: Redefining the Subject in Caribbean Literature." *Kunapipi* 11, no. 1 (1989): 17–26.

———. "Marvellous Realism—The Way out of Negritude." *Caribbean Studies* 13, no. 4 (1974): 57–70.

Davies, Carole Boyce, and Elaine Savory Fido, ed. *Out of the Kumbla: Caribbean Women and Literature.* Trenton, N.J.: Africa World Press, 1990.

Dayan, Joan. "Caribbean Cannibals and Whores." *Raritan* 9, no. 2 (Fall 1989): 45–67.

———. "Vodoun, or the Voice of the Gods." *Raritan* 10, no. 3 (Winter 1991): 32–57.

de Certeau, Michel. *Heterologies: Discourse on the Other.* Trans. Brian Massumi. Minneapolis: University of Minnesota Press, 1986.

———. *The Writing of History.* Trans. Tom Conley. New York: Columbia University Press, 1988.

de Man, Paul. *Allegories of Reading: Figural Language in Rousseau, Nietzsche, Rilke and Proust.* New Haven, Conn.: Yale University Press, 1979.

Deren, Maya. *Divine Horsemen: The Living Gods of Haiti*. New York: Thames and Hudson, 1953.

Edgell, Zee. *Beka Lamb*. London: Heinemann, 1982.

Eliot, T. S. *The Complete Poems and Plays, 1909–1950*. San Diego: Harcourt Brace Jovanovich, 1952.

The Empire Strikes Back: Race and Racism in Seventies Britain. 1982. Reprint, London: Hutchinson and the Centre for Contemporary Cultural Studies in Birmingham, 1983.

Fanon, Frantz. *The Wretched of the Earth*. Trans. Constance Farrington. Middlesex, England: Penguin, 1963.

———. *Black Skin, White Masks*. Trans. Charles Lam Markmann. New York: Grove Press, 1967.

———. *Toward the African Revolution: Political Essays*. Trans. Haakon Chevalier. New York: Grove Press, 1967.

Fineman, Joel. "The Structure of Allegorical Desire." In *Allegory and Representation*, ed. Stephen J. Greenblatt, 26–60. Baltimore: Johns Hopkins University Press, 1981.

Froude, James Anthony. *The English in the West Indies, or the Bow of Ulysses*. London: Longmans, Green and Co., 1888.

Gates, Henry Louis, Jr., ed. *"Race," Writing and Difference*. Chicago: Chicago University Press, 1986.

———. "Critical Fanonism." *Critical Inquiry* 17 (Spring 1991): 457–70.

Genovese, Eugene D. *Roll, Jordan, Roll: The World the Slaves Made*. 1972. Reprint, New York: Vintage, 1976.

Gikandi, Simon. *Writing in Limbo: Modernism and Caribbean Literature*. Ithaca, N.Y.: Cornell University Press, 1992.

Gilman, Sander. *Difference and Pathology: Stereotypes of Sexuality, Race and Madness*. Ithaca, N.Y.: Cornell University Press, 1985.

Gilroy, Paul. *The Black Atlantic: Modernity and Double Consciousness*. Cambridge, Mass.: Harvard University Press, 1993.

———. *Small Acts: Thoughts on the Politics of Black Cultures*. London: Serpent's Tail, 1993.

Glissant, Edouard. *Caribbean Discourse: Selected Essays*. Translated with an introduction by J. Michael Dash. Charlottesville: University Press of Virginia, 1989.

Gmelch, George. *Double Passage: The Lives of Caribbean Migrants Abroad and Back Home*. Ann Arbor: University of Michigan Press, 1992.

Gramsci, Antonio. *Selections from the Prison Notebooks*. Trans. Quintin Hoare and Geoffrey Nowell Smith. New York: International Publishers, 1971.

———. *Selections from Political Writings, 1910–1920*. Ed. Quintin Hoare, trans. John Mathews. Minneapolis: University of Minneapolis Press, 1977.

———. "National-Popular Literature, The Popular Novel and Observations on Folklore." In *Communication and Class Struggle*, ed. Armand Mattelart and Seth Siegelaub, 71–75. Vol 2. New York: International General, 1983.

Green, Martin. *Dreams of Adventure, Deeds of Empire*. New York: Basic Books, 1979.

Griswold, Wendy. "The Fabrication of Meaning: Literary Interpretation in the United States, Great Britain and the West Indies." *American Journal of Sociology* 92, no. 5 (1987): 1077–1117.

Hakluyt, Richard. *The Principal Navigations, Voyages, Traffiques, and Discoveries of the English Nation*. 12 vols. Glasgow: MacLehose, 1903–5.

Hall, Stuart. "On Postmodernism and Articulation." Interview by Lawrence Grossberg et al. *Journal of Communication Inquiry* 10, no. 2 (Summer 1986): 45–60.

———. "Cultural Identity and Diaspora." In *Identity: Community, Culture, Difference*, ed. J. Rutherford, 222–37. London: Lawrence and Wishart, 1990.

Hanchard, Michael. "Racial Consciousness and Afro-Diasporic Experiences: Antonio Gramsci Reconsidered." *Socialism and Democracy* 7, no. 3 (1991): 83–106.

Harlow, Barbara. *Resistance Literature*. New York: Methuen, 1987.

Harlow, Vincent T. *A History of Barbados, 1625–1685*. Oxford: Clarendon Press, 1926.

Harris, Wilson. *Tradition, the Writer and Society: Critical Essays*. London: New Beacon, 1967.

———. *History, Fable and Myth in the Caribbean and Guianas*. Georgetown, Guyana: The National History and Arts Council and the Ministry of Information and Culture, 1970.

———. *The Radical Imagination: Lectures and Talks*. Ed. Alan Riach and Mark Williams. Belgium: L³—Liege, Language and Literature, 1992.

Hegel, G. W. F. *Lectures on the Philosophy of History*. Trans. J. Sibree. New York: Henry G. Bohn, 1857.

Helgerson, Richard. "Camões, Hakluyt, and the Voyages of Two Nations." In *Colonialism and Culture*, ed. Nicholas B. Dirks. Ann Arbor: University of Michigan Press, 1992.

Herskovits, Melville J. *Life in a Haitian Valley*. Introduction by Kamau Brathwaite. New York: Anchor Doubleday, 1971.

Hiro, Dilip. *Black British, White British: A History of Race Relations in Britain*. 1971. Reprint, London: Grafton, 1991.

Hobsbawm, Eric, and Terence Ranger. *The Invention of Tradition*. Cambridge, England: Cambridge University Press, 1983.

Hodge, Merle. *Crick Crack, Monkey*. London: Heinemann, 1970.

hooks, bell. *Yearning: Race, Gender and Cultural Politics*. Boston: South End Press, 1990.

Hulme, Peter. *Colonial Encounters: Europe and the Native Caribbean, 1492–1797*. 1986. Reprint, London: Routledge, 1992.

Hurbon, Laënnec. "Vodou: A Faith for Individual, Family, and Community from *Dieu dans le vaudou haitien*." *Callaloo* 15, no. 3 (1992): 787–96.

Hurston, Zora Neale. *Tell My Horse: Voodoo and Life in Haiti and Jamaica*. Afterword by Henry Louis Gates, Jr. 1938. Reprint, New York: Harper and Row, 1990.

James, C. L. R. *The Black Jacobins: Toussaint L'Ouverture and the San Domingo Revolution*. Rev. ed., with an appendix by C. L. R. James, New York: Vintage, 1989.

———. *Beyond a Boundary*. 1963. Reprint, Durham: Duke University Press, 1993.

James, Winston, and Clive Harris, ed. *Inside Babylon: The Caribbean Diaspora in Britain*. London: Verso, 1993.

Jameson, Fredric. "Third-World Literature in the Era of Multinational Capitalism." *Social Text* 15 (1986): 65–88.

Jonas, Joyce. *Anancy in the Great House: Ways of Reading West Indian Fiction*. New York: Greenwood Press, 1990.

Knight, Franklin W. *The Caribbean: The Genesis of a Fragmented Nationalism*. 2d ed. New York: Oxford University Press, 1990.

Knight, Franklin W., and Colin A. Palmer, ed. *The Modern Caribbean*. Chapel Hill, N.C.: The University of North Carolina Press, 1989.

Laguerre, Michel S. *Voodoo and Politics in Haiti*. New York: St. Martin's Press, 1989.

Lamming, George. *In the Castle of My Skin*. 1953. Reprint, with an introduction by George Lamming and a foreword by Sandra Pouchet Paquet, Ann Arbor: University of Michigan Press, 1991.

———. *The Emigrants*. 1954. Reprint, Ann Arbor: University of Michigan Press, 1994.

———. *Of Age and Innocence*. 1958. Reprint, London: Allison and Busby, 1981.

———. *Season of Adventure*. 1960. Reprint, London: Allison and Busby, 1979.

———. *The Pleasures of Exile*. 1960. Reprint, with a foreword by Sandra Pouchet Paquet, Ann Arbor: University of Michigan Press, 1992.

———. *Water With Berries*. 1971. Reprint, London: Longman Caribbean, 1973.

———. *Natives of My Person*. 1972. Reprint, Ann Arbor: University of Michigan Press, 1992.

———. "Address to the Jamaica Press Association Meeting." In *George Lamming et le Destin des Caraibes* by Ambroise Kom. 263–73. Quebec: Didier, 1986.

———. *Conversations: George Lamming Essays, Addresses and Interviews, 1953–1990*. Ed. Richard Drayton and Andaiye. London: Karia Press, 1992.

Laroche, Maximilien. "Music, Dance, Religion." Trans. Paulette Richards. *Callaloo* 15, no.3 (1992): 797–810.

Lent, John A., ed. *Caribbean Popular Culture*. Bowling Green, Ohio: Bowling Green State University Press, 1990.

Lewis, Gordon K. *The Growth of the Modern West Indies*. New York: Monthly Review Press, 1968.

Lewis, William Arthur. *Labour in the West Indies: The Birth of a Worker's Movement*. London: Fabian Society, 1939.

Ligon, Richard. *A True and Exact History of Barbados*. London: Humphrey Moseley, 1657.

Lindfors, Bernth. "The West Indian Conference in Commonwealth Literature." *World Literature Written in English* 19 (1971): 9–13.

Lukács, Georg. *The Historical Novel*. Trans. H. and S. Mitchell. London: Merlin, 1962.

———. "Reification and the Consciousness of the Proletariat." In *History and Class Consciousness: Studies in Marxist Dialectics*. Trans. Rodney Livingstone, 83–222. Cambridge, Mass.: MIT Press, 1971.

———. *The Theory of the Novel: A Historico-Philosophical Essay on the Forms of Great Epic Literature*. Trans. Anna Bostock. Cambridge, Mass.: MIT Press, 1971.

Mannix, Daniel P., and Malcolm Cowley. *Black Cargoes: A History of the Atlantic Slave Trade, 1518–1865*. New York: Viking, 1962.

Mannoni, Dominique O. *Prospero and Caliban: The Psychology of Colonization*. Trans. Pamela Powesland. London: Methuen, 1956.

Marable, Manning. *African and Caribbean Politics from Kwame Nkrumah to the Grenada Revolution*. London: Verso, 1987.

Marx, Karl. *Capital: A Critique of Political Economy*. Trans. Ben Fowkes. Vol. 1. New York: Vintage, 1976.

Mercer, Kobena. *Welcome to the Jungle: New Positions in Black Cultural Studies*. New York: Routledge, 1994.

Mintz, Sidney, ed. *Slavery, Colonialism, and Racism*. New York: W. W. Norton, 1974.

Munro, Ian, and Reinhard Sander, ed. *Kas-Kas: Interviews with Three Caribbean Writers in Texas: George Lamming, C. L. R. James, Wilson Harris.* Austin, Texas: African and Afro-American Research Institute, 1972.

Naipaul, V. S. *The Middle Passage: Impressions of Five Societies—British, French and Dutch—in the West Indies and South America.* 1962. Reprint, New York: Vintage, 1981.

Nasta, Susheila, ed. *Motherlands: Black Women's Writing from Africa, the Caribbean, and South Asia.* 1991. Reprint, New Brunswick, N.J.: Rutgers University Press, 1992.

Ngũgĩ, wa Thiong'o. *Homecoming: Essays on African and Caribbean Literature, Culture and Politics.* London: Heinemann, 1972.

———. *Decolonising the Mind: The Politics of Language in African Literature.* London: James Currey, 1986.

Nixon, Rob. "Caribbean and African Appropriations of *The Tempest.*" *Critical Inquiry* 13 (Spring 1987): 557–78.

———. *London Calling: V. S. Naipaul, Postcolonial Mandarin.* New York: Oxford University Press, 1992.

Paquet, Sandra Pouchet. *The Novels of George Lamming.* London: Heinemann, 1982.

Parris, Ronald Glenfield. *Race, Inequality and Underdevelopment in Barbados, 1627–1973.* Ann Arbor: University Microfilms, 1974.

Phillips, Caryl. *The Final Passage.* New York: Penguin, 1985.

Poyer, John. *The History of Barbados from the First Discovery of the Island in the Year 1605 till the Accession of Lord Seaforth 1801.* 1808. Reprint, London: Frank Cass, 1971.

Prakash, Gyan, ed. *After Colonialism: Imperial Histories and Postcolonial Displacements.* Princeton, N.J.: Princeton University Press, 1995.

Pratt, Mary Louise. *Imperial Eyes: Travel Writing and Transculturation.* London: Routledge, 1992.

Puckrein, Gary A. *Little England: Plantation Society and Anglo-Barbadian Politics, 1627–1700.* New York: New York University Press, 1984.

Ramchand, Kenneth. *The West Indian Novel and its Background.* 2d ed. London: Heinemann, 1983.

Retamar, Roberto Fernandez. "Caliban: Notes Toward a Discussion of Culture in our America." Trans. Lynn Garafola et al. *The Massachussets Review* 15, nos. 1–2 (Winter–Spring 1974): 7–72.

———. "Caliban Revisited." In *Caliban and Other Essays,* trans. Edward Baker, 46–55. Minneapolis: University of Minnesota Press, 1989.

Robinson, Gillian, and John Rundell, ed. *Rethinking Imagination: Culture and Creativity.* London: Routledge, 1994.

Rodney, Walter. *How Europe Underdeveloped Africa.* Washington, D. C.: Howard University Press, 1974.

Rohlehr, Gordon. "The Folk in Caribbean Literature." In *Critical Perspectives on Sam Selvon,* ed. Susheila Nasta. 29–43. Washington, D.C.: Three Continents Press, 1988.

Said, Edward. *Culture and Imperialism.* New York: Alfred A. Knopf, 1993.

Sander, Reinhard. *From Trinidad: An Anthology of Early West Indian Writing.* New York: Africana Publishing Co., 1978.

———. *The Trinidad Awakening: West Indian Literature of the Nineteen-Thirties.* New York: Greenwood Press, 1988.

Sangari, Kumkum. "The Politics of the Possible." *Cultural Critique* 7 (Fall 1987): 157–86.

Scott, James C. *Domination and the Arts of Resistance: Hidden Transcripts.* New Haven: Yale University Press, 1990.

Shakespeare, William. *The Tempest.* In *The Riverside Shakespeare,* ed. G. Blakemore Evans, 1611–38. Boston: Houghton Mifflin, 1974.

Sharp, Buchanan. *In Contempt of All Authority: Rural Artisans and Riot in the West of England, 1586–1660.* Berkeley: University of California Press, 1980.

Sivanandan, Ambalavaner. *A Different Hunger: Writings on Black Resistance.* London: Pluto, 1982.

Slemon, Stephen. "Monuments of Empire: Allegory/Counter-Discourse/Post-colonial Writing." *Kunapipi* 9, no. 3 (1987): 1–16.

———. "Post-Colonial Allegory and the Transformation of History." *Journal of Commonwealth Literature* 23, no. 1 (1988): 157–68.

Smith, Faith L. "Coming Home to the Real Thing: Gender and Intellectual Life in the Anglophone Caribbean." *South Atlantic Quarterly* 93, no. 4 (Fall 1994): 895–923.

Smith, Paul. "The Will to Allegory in Postmodernism." *Dalhousie Review* 62, no. 1 (Spring 1982): 105–22.

Solomos, John. *Race and Racism in Contemporary Britain.* London: Macmillan, 1989.

Spivak, Gayatri Chakravorty. "Can the Subaltern Speak?" In *Marxism and the Interpretation of Culture,* ed. Cary Nelson and Lawrence Grossberg, 271–313. Urbana: University of Illinois Press, 1988.

Taussig, Michael T. *The Devil and Commodity Fetishism in South America.* Chapel Hill, N.C.: University of North Carolina Press, 1980.

Taylor, Patrick. *The Narrative of Liberation: Perspectives on Afro-Caribbean Literature, Popular Culture and Politics.* Ithaca, N.Y.: Cornell University Press, 1989.

———. "Anthropology and Theology in Pursuit of Justice." *Callaloo* 15, no. 3 (1992): 811–23.

Thomas-Hope, Elizabeth M. "Caribbean Diaspora, The Inheritance of Slavery: Migration from the Commonwealth Caribbean." In *The Caribbean in Europe: Aspects of the West Indian Experience in Britain, France and the Netherlands,* ed. Colin Brock, 15–35. London: Frank Cass, 1986.

Trollope, Anthony. *The West Indies and the Spanish Main.* New York: Harper and Brothers, 1860.

Veeser, Aram H., ed. *The New Historicism.* New York: Routledge, 1989.

Walcott, Derek. "What the Twilight Says: An Overture." In *Dream on Monkey Mountain and Other Plays,* 3–27. New York: Farrar, Straus and Giroux, 1970.

———. "The Muse of History." In *Is Massa Day Dead? Black Moods in the Caribbean,* ed. Orde Coombes, 1–27. New York: Anchor/Doubleday, 1974.

———. *The Antilles: Fragments of Epic Memory.* The Nobel Lecture. New York: Farrar, Straus and Giroux, 1992.

Walker, Alice. *In Search of Our Mother's Gardens.* San Diego: Harcourt Brace Jovanovich, 1983.

Weekes, Nathaniel. "Barbados." In *The Penguin Book of Caribbean Verse in English,* ed. Paula Burnett, 102–3. Middlesex, England: Penguin, 1986.

Williams, Eric. *British Historians and the West Indies.* London: Andre Deutsch, 1966.

———. *From Columbus to Castro: The History of the Caribbean, 1492–1969.* 1970. Reprint, New York: Vintage, 1984.

————, ed. *Documents of West Indian History, 1492–1655*. Vol. 1. Trinidad: PNM Publishing Co., 1963.

Williams, Raymond. *Marxism and Literature*. Oxford: Oxford University Press, 1977.

Wynter, Sylvia. *The Hills of Hebron*. Essex, England: Longman, 1966.

————. "We Must Learn to Sit Down Together and Talk about a Little Culture: Reflections on West Indian Writing and Criticism. Part One." *Jamaica Journal* 2 (December 1968): 24–32.

Yarde, Gloria. "George Lamming: The Historical Imagination." *The Literary Half-Yearly* 11, no. 2 (1970): 35–45.

Index

167